Disclaimer

The information in this book, Financial Forensics Unleashed: Empowering Entrepreneurs, CEOs, Auditors, and Financial Experts to Detect and Prevent Fraud, is intended for educational and informational purposes only and does not serve as legal, financial, or professional advice specific to any individual or organisation.

While every effort has been made to ensure the accuracy and reliability of the content at the time of publication, the author and publisher make no representations or warranties, express or implied, regarding the completeness, accuracy, or suitability of the information contained herein. Laws, regulations, and professional practices are subject to change and may vary by jurisdiction.

The reader is advised to consult with qualified professionals, such as certified accountants, legal advisors, or auditors, before making decisions based on the concepts, examples, or case studies presented in this book. The author and publisher disclaim any liability for loss or damage, whether direct or indirect, arising from using or applying any information in this publication.

Any names, organisations, or scenarios used in case studies or examples are fictionalised or generalised unless otherwise stated, and any resemblance to real persons or entities is purely coincidental.

FINANCIAL FORENSICS UNLEASHED

EMPOWERING ENTREPRENEURS, CEOS, AUDITORS, AND FINANCIAL EXPERTS TO DETECT AND PREVENT FRAUD

CA SATISH PATEL

Copyright © CA Satish Patel 2025
All Rights Reserved.

ISBN
Hardcase 979-8-89984-317-4
Paperback 979-8-89929-366-5

This book has been published with all efforts taken to make the material error-free after the consent of the author. However, the author and the publisher do not assume and hereby disclaim any liability to any party for any loss, damage, or disruption caused by errors or omissions, whether such errors or omissions result from negligence, accident, or any other cause.

While every effort has been made to avoid any mistake or omission, this publication is being sold on the condition and understanding that neither the author nor the publishers or printers would be liable in any manner to any person by reason of any mistake or omission in this publication or for any action taken or omitted to be taken or advice rendered or accepted on the basis of this work. For any defect in printing or binding the publishers will be liable only to replace the defective copy by another copy of this work then available.

Dedication

I want to express my gratitude to my family for their unwavering support, encouragement, and patience throughout this journey.

To my colleagues and mentors, thank you for your guidance and wisdom, which have profoundly shaped my path in forensic accounting.

Lastly, this book is dedicated to all professionals committed to upholding integrity, transparency, and truth in finance. May it empower you to make a meaningful impact and safeguard the financial world.

Contents

Part 4: The Future of Forensic Accounting

Preface

In today's dynamic business world, organisations face countless challenges in protecting their financial assets and maintaining their reputations. As digital transactions, global business networks, and sophisticated financial crimes proliferate, the need for rigorous, proactive fraud prevention has never been greater. This book, *Financial Forensics Unleashed: Empowering Entrepreneurs, CEOs, Auditors, and Financial Experts to Detect and Prevent Fraud*, was born out of a vision to equip business leaders, forensic accountants, consultants, and financial professionals with the tools and insights to meet these challenges head-on.

Over the past three decades, I have witnessed firsthand the evolution of financial fraud and the growing complexity of detecting and preventing it. I've worked with businesses of all sizes, from local enterprises to corporations, each with unique vulnerabilities and risk profiles. These experiences have taught me the critical role forensic accounting plays in uncovering fraud and helping organisations build resilient systems that foster transparency, accountability, and trust.

This book is a comprehensive guide, structured to take readers through the fundamentals of forensic accounting, the techniques used to detect and investigate fraud, and the applications that can safeguard businesses. Whether you are a business owner looking to establish sound financial practices, a forensic accountant seeking to expand your skill set, or a consultant advising clients on risk management, you will find practical insights here to support your goals.

The book is divided into four main sections. Part 1, *Fundamentals of Forensic Accounting*, provides foundational knowledge, explaining the key principles, ethical considerations, and professional requirements that define forensic accounting. Part 2, *Techniques and Tools in Forensic Accounting*, dives into the investigative methods and technologies that enable forensic accountants to detect fraud and gather evidence. This includes analytical tools, data collection methods, and interviewing techniques essential for effective investigations.

In Part 3, *Applications of Forensic Accounting*, we explore real-world scenarios in which forensic accounting plays a vital role. These include corporate governance, financial crime investigations, and litigation support. Case studies are used throughout to bring these concepts to life, allowing readers to see the tangible impact of forensic accounting on preventing and addressing financial misconduct.

Finally, Part 4, *The Future of Forensic Accounting*, looks forward to emerging trends and the evolving role of forensic accountants. With digital currencies, AI, and blockchain reshaping the industry, forensic accountants must adapt to new challenges and embrace new tools to remain effective. This final section encourages readers to stay vigilant, ethical, and adaptable in their careers.

The journey to write this book has been driven by a desire to create a practical resource that imparts knowledge and inspires action. I hope this book empowers readers to take an active role in preventing financial fraud, protecting organisational assets, and supporting the integrity of our financial systems. Financial forensic accounting is not just a profession but a critical field that safeguards the economic foundation upon which businesses and communities thrive.

I want to thank all my colleagues, clients, and mentors who have contributed to my knowledge and understanding of forensic accounting.

I am also profoundly grateful to my family for their support and patience throughout the writing process.

This book is dedicated to all those who strive to uphold honesty and integrity in business. May it be a valuable companion in your pursuit of truth, accountability, and financial security.

Indore

May 21, 2025

– **CA Satish Patel**

Foreword

In an era marked by unprecedented economic growth, rapid technological innovation, and intricate financial systems, businesses' demand for accountability and transparency has soared. As organisations expand globally, the complexity of financial crimes and fraud escalates. In this context, the role of the forensic accountant stands out, becoming indispensable as both a fraud detector and a guardian of financial integrity.

"Financial Forensics Unleashed: Empowering Entrepreneurs, CEOs, Auditors, and Financial Experts to Detect and Prevent Fraud" is a timely and insightful book that addresses these critical challenges. Backed by three decades of expertise in accounting, auditing, and financial consulting, the author provides invaluable knowledge, presenting a comprehensive guide for current and aspiring forensic accountants, business owners, consultants, and financial professionals aiming to protect their organisations from fraud.

This book meticulously covers the fundamentals of forensic accounting, including foundational principles and advanced investigative techniques. It offers a clear and practical roadmap for understanding and preventing financial fraud, addressing topics ranging from data analytics and interviewing techniques to applying emerging technologies like blockchain and AI in investigations. Readers gain firsthand insights into real-world scenarios through well-chosen case studies, illustrating how forensic accounting can uncover complex schemes and help organisations respond effectively to financial threats. This practical approach ensures that readers feel equipped and ready to apply the knowledge they gain from this book.

What distinguishes this book is its emphasis on proactive approaches in forensic accounting. Instead of just reacting to fraud, the author advocates for the establishment of robust internal controls and the cultivation of a culture of transparency and ethical behaviour. This proactive approach is particularly crucial in today's business environment, where timely action can make the difference between safeguarding assets and suffering irreparable financial damage. By focusing on prevention, the author empowers readers to develop and implement systems designed to deter fraud before it can harm their organisations.

Moreover, the book addresses the evolving landscape of forensic accounting, highlighting both the opportunities and challenges of technological advancements and digital currencies. As financial systems become increasingly digitised, the toolkit for forensic accountants must also evolve. The author skillfully navigates these developments, offering practical advice on leveraging cutting-edge tools while discussing the ethical considerations that should guide forensic accounting in a digital age.

This book, 'Financial Forensics Unleashed', is more than a technical manual; it serves as a guide to strengthening organisations' financial integrity and supporting long-term, sustainable success. It will be an invaluable resource for business leaders, startups, auditors, consultants, and anyone committed to upholding the highest standards of transparency and accountability in finance. Your interest and engagement with this book are integral to the field of forensic accounting, and we value your contribution to this important work.

I am confident that readers will find this book indispensable, equipping them with the knowledge and skills necessary to excel in forensic accounting. Whether you are an experienced professional or new to the field, this book will challenge you to think critically, act ethically, and make a lasting impact in the fight against financial fraud.

Ahmadabad

May 20, 2025

– **Mr. P S PATEL**

Chairman & Managing Director

PSP Project Limited

Introduction

Who is the Forensic Accountant and Auditor?

Forensic accounting and auditing are essential fields in today's complex financial landscape. With the growing prevalence of financial fraud, regulatory requirements, and high-profile corporate scandals, forensic accountants and auditors are at the forefront, working to uncover hidden financial risks, prevent fraud, and protect organisational assets. But who exactly are these forensic accountants and auditors, and what makes their role so critical?

A forensic accountant is a highly specialised professional who combines accounting expertise with investigative skills to detect, examine, and document financial inconsistencies, often concerning legal matters. Unlike traditional accountants, who primarily focus on recording and managing financial data, forensic accountants delve into the details, searching for patterns, anomalies, and inconsistencies that may indicate fraudulent activity. Forensic accountants approach each case with a detective's mindset, guided by analytical rigour and a commitment to integrity, whether investigating embezzlement, tracing the flow of funds in a money-laundering scheme, or assisting in divorce settlements.

Forensic auditors play a similar yet distinct role. While they, too, possess accounting skills and investigative abilities, forensic auditors often focus on internal controls, compliance, and ensuring that an organisation's financial practices align with regulatory standards and ethical guidelines. They evaluate an organisation's systems, procedures, and documentation to ensure that monetary transactions are transparent, legitimate, and accurately recorded. Forensic auditors may work closely with corporate boards, management, and regulatory bodies to recommend strategies for improving financial security and preventing fraud before it happens.

Characteristics and Skills of Forensic Accountants and Auditors

Forensic accountants and auditors possess unique characteristics and skills that distinguish them from other financial professionals. Some of these include:

Attention to Detail: Financial crimes are often concealed within complex data. Forensic professionals meticulously examine documents, records, and transactions to uncover subtle clues.

Analytical and Investigative Mindset: Beyond traditional accounting, forensic accountants and auditors approach their work like detectives, piecing together information to construct narratives from financial data that may reveal misconduct.

Legal Knowledge: Since their work frequently intersects with the legal system, forensic accountants and auditors need a solid understanding of relevant laws, regulations, and legal standards.

Ethical Integrity: Forensic accountants and auditors must uphold the highest ethical standards. Their findings can have significant legal and financial implications, making accuracy, honesty, and impartiality essential.

Communication Skills: Forensic professionals must effectively convey complex financial information clearly and concisely, often in high-stakes environments such as courtrooms or boardrooms

The Growing Demand for Forensic Accounting and Auditing

The need for forensic accounting and auditing has grown exponentially in recent years. Corporate fraud, cybercrimes, and financial misstatements have become more sophisticated and frequent. In response, businesses, regulators, and governments have increasingly turned to forensic accountants and auditors to provide clarity, transparency, and accountability. Financial scandals, whether involving global corporations or small businesses, highlight the vulnerabilities within financial systems and the critical role of forensic professionals in safeguarding financial integrity.

In addition, as businesses expand into international markets and adopt digital payment systems, new forms of fraud, such as cryptocurrency scams and cyberattacks, have emerged. Forensic accountants and auditors must continually adapt to these new challenges by leveraging advanced tools and methodologies, including data analytics, blockchain analysis, and AI-driven fraud detection. Their work has become more interdisciplinary, often requiring collaboration with IT experts, legal advisors, and cybersecurity professionals.

Purpose of This Book

This book is a comprehensive guide for those who wish to understand, develop, and apply forensic accounting and auditing principles. Whether you are a business owner aiming to protect your organisation, a financial professional seeking to expand your skill set, or a student exploring career paths, this book provides the essential knowledge, tools, and insights to succeed in this field.

The following chapters will introduce you to the core concepts of forensic accounting, essential investigative techniques, and real-world applications across various industries. You will gain a deeper understanding of the forensic accountant and auditor's role and the proactive steps organisations can take to prevent fraud, protect assets, and create a culture of integrity.

In today's complex world, forensic accountants and auditors are more than just financial experts—they are guardians of trust, transparency, and ethical financial practices. Their work ensures that businesses operate responsibly and that financial transactions reflect truth and integrity. By the end of this book, you will understand who these professionals are and what they do and be inspired to uphold the values of forensic accounting and auditing in all financial endeavours.

Welcome to the forensic accounting and auditing world, where finance meets investigation and integrity drives success.

Unveiling the Hidden Truths

Forensic accounting, a specialised field that blends financial expertise with investigative techniques, has become crucial in today's complex financial landscape. This discipline delves into the intricate world of financial records, unravelling fraud, corruption, and other financial irregularities. By employing a meticulous approach, forensic accountants play a pivotal role in safeguarding businesses, protecting investors, and ensuring the integrity of financial systems.

Overview of Forensic Accounting

At its core, forensic accounting involves the application of accounting, auditing, and investigative skills to identify, analyse, and interpret financial data. Forensic accountants possess a keen eye for detail and a deep understanding of financial principles. They meticulously examine financial records, scrutinise transactions, and identify patterns or anomalies that may indicate fraudulent or illegal activities.

The Importance of Forensic Accounting in Modern Finance

In an era characterised by rapid globalisation and technological advancements, the risks of financial misconduct have escalated. Forensic accounting has become indispensable in addressing these challenges. Here are some key reasons why forensic accounting is crucial in modern finance:

- Detecting and Preventing Fraud: Forensic accountants employ advanced techniques to uncover fraudulent schemes, such as embezzlement, money laundering, and accounting fraud. Their insights enable organisations to implement robust internal controls and safeguards to mitigate the risk of future financial crimes.
- Resolving Financial Disputes: When disputes arise over financial matters, forensic accountants provide expert testimony and analysis to support legal proceedings. Their objective findings help courts and arbitrators make informed decisions.
- Enforcing Regulatory Compliance: As regulatory frameworks become increasingly stringent, forensic accountants assist organisations in adhering to compliance standards. They identify potential compliance gaps and develop strategies to mitigate risks.
- Mitigating Risk and Loss: Forensic accountants help organisations minimise potential losses by proactively identifying and addressing financial risks. Their expertise enables businesses to make informed decisions and safeguard their assets.

In the following chapters, we will explore the various facets of forensic accounting, exploring its methodologies, applications, and the challenges faced by practitioners in this dynamic field. By understanding the intricacies of forensic accounting, we can better appreciate its significance in safeguarding the financial health of individuals, businesses, and society.

The Evolution of Forensic Accounting

While the term "forensic accounting" is relatively recent, using financial expertise to investigate and resolve disputes has a long history.

Ancient Roots

The origins of forensic accounting can be traced back to ancient civilisations. Historical texts, scriptures, and administrative records from ancient India indicate that financial oversight, fraud detection, and accountability mechanisms were integral to governance. Some of the earliest references to forensic accounting principles can be found in ancient Indian scriptures like the **Arthashastra** by **Chanakya (Kautilya)**, who served as the chief advisor to Emperor **Chandragupta Maurya (321–297 BCE)**.

Forensic accounting in ancient India was not just a theoretical concept but a well-documented practice in governance, taxation, trade, and temple finances. The principles outlined in the **Arthashastra**, combined with the financial administration practices of the **Maurya and Gupta Empires**, laid the foundation for financial oversight and fraud detection. These early Indian practices closely align with modern forensic accounting, proving that financial accountability and fraud prevention have been essential aspects of governance since ancient times.

Ancient Egyptians, for instance, employed scribes to record financial transactions on papyrus scrolls meticulously. This practice served as a form of internal control to prevent fraud and ensure accurate record-keeping. Similarly, the Roman Empire had officials known as "cognitors" responsible for managing financial disputes and verifying the authenticity of financial records.

The Modern Era

The modern era of forensic accounting began to take shape in the early 20th century. The need for specialised financial investigators became more apparent with the increasing complexity of financial transactions and the rise of white-collar crime. A pivotal moment in the history of forensic accounting came in the 1930s when Frank Wilson, a CPA working for the U.S. Internal Revenue Service, was tasked with investigating the financial dealings of Al Capone. Wilson's successful use of accounting techniques to build a strong case against Capone marked a significant milestone in the development of forensic accounting.

Post-World War II

The post-World War II era witnessed a surge in economic activity and globalisation, leading to increased financial fraud and corruption. This period saw the emergence of professional organisations dedicated to forensic accounting, such as the Association of Certified Fraud Examiners (ACFE). These organisations played a crucial role in establishing standards of practice, promoting ethical conduct, and advancing the field through research and education.

The Enron Era and Beyond

The collapse of Enron and WorldCom in the early 2000s exposed significant corporate fraud and accounting scandals, further highlighting the importance of forensic accounting. These high-profile cases led to increased regulatory scrutiny and a renewed focus on corporate governance. Forensic accountants became essential in investigating these scandals, identifying fraudulent activities, and quantifying financial losses.

The Digital Age

In recent years, the rapid advancement of technology has transformed the landscape of forensic accounting. Digital evidence, such as emails, spreadsheets, and databases, has become increasingly important in investigations. Forensic accountants must now possess a strong understanding of computer forensics and data analytics to extract and analyse digital information effectively.

Key Developments in Forensic Accounting:

- Increased Specialisation: Forensic accountants now specialise in various areas, such as fraud examination, litigation support, and business valuation.
- Advancement of Technology: The use of sophisticated software tools and techniques has enhanced the efficiency and accuracy of forensic investigations.
- Global Collaboration: Forensic accountants collaborate across borders to investigate complex international fraud schemes.
- Emphasis on Prevention: Forensic accountants are increasingly involved in designing and implementing fraud prevention programs.

As the financial world continues to evolve, forensic accounting will remain a vital tool for detecting, preventing, and investigating financial crime. By staying abreast of emerging trends and technologies, forensic accountants will continue to play a crucial role in safeguarding the integrity of financial systems.

Part 1

Fundamentals of Forensic Accounting

Chapter 01

What is Forensic Accounting?

"Beyond the Balance Sheet: The Strategic Importance of Forensic Accounting"

Definition and Overview

Forensic accounting is defined as the application of accounting and investigative techniques to uncover, document, and resolve financial disputes and fraud. It involves examining and verifying financial information to detect discrepancies, fraudulent activities, or compliance breaches. Forensic accountants play a crucial role in legal proceedings by providing expert testimony and helping to quantify damages.

Unlike traditional accounting, which focuses primarily on recording and reporting financial transactions, forensic accounting delves deeper into uncovering, analysing, and interpreting financial data in cases of potential fraud, disputes, or irregularities. This field combines accounting, auditing, and investigative skills to address financial crimes, resolve conflicts, and support legal proceedings.

Forensic accounting is a specialised field that combines investigative and auditing skills to analyse financial information for many purposes. It is often referred to as the "financial detective work" required to uncover fraud, embezzlement, or financial irregularities.

The term *forensic* indicates that the work is suitable for presentation in court, emphasising the legal applicability of the findings.

Definition:

Definition of Forensic Accounting

1. **General Definition**

   "Forensic accounting involves the use of accounting, auditing, and investigative skills to examine financial records and transactions to resolve disputes or detect fraud"

2. **Legal Definition**

   "Forensic accounting refers to the practice of preparing financial information in a manner that is admissible in legal proceedings, whether for litigation, criminal cases, or regulatory inquiries."

3. **Practical Definition**

   "It's the art and science of investigating financial data to uncover fraud, errors, or omissions and to ensure transparency and accountability in financial systems."

Scope of Forensic Accounting

The scope of forensic accounting is vast and continually expanding with advancements in technology and the complexity of financial crimes. Below are the primary areas of focus:

1. **Fraud Detection and Prevention**

   - Identifying and investigating fraud cases, such as embezzlement, falsified records, or misappropriation of funds.
   - Developing systems and controls to prevent fraudulent activities.

2. **Litigation Support**

   - Assisting legal teams with financial expertise during disputes.

> Preparing evidence, analysing financial statements, and providing expert testimony in court.

3. **Corporate Governance and Internal Controls**

> Ensuring compliance with regulations and laws through audits and risk assessments.

> Recommending improvements to governance structures to minimise risk.

4. **Money Laundering Investigations**

> Tracing illicit funds through complex layers of transactions.

> Assisting law enforcement in compliance with anti-money laundering laws like PMLA (Prevention of Money Laundering Act).

5. **Bankruptcy and Insolvency Investigations**

> Identifying fraudulent transfers, asset misappropriation, and hidden liabilities during bankruptcy proceedings.

> Supporting creditors and courts in resolving disputes.

6. **Insurance Claims and Disputes**

> Validating insurance claims by analysing financial records to determine their legitimacy.

> Investigating fraudulent claims or exaggerated losses.

7. **Cyber Forensics and Digital Fraud**

> Investigating fraud in digital environments, including online banking fraud, cryptocurrency scams, and identity theft.

> Collecting and preserving electronic evidence.

8. **Valuation Disputes**

> Resolving disputes related to asset valuation, such as business mergers, acquisitions, or divorce settlements.

Key Characteristics of Forensic Accounting

1. **Investigative Nature**

   ➢ Goes beyond traditional accounting to uncover hidden facts.

   ➢ Requires a proactive approach to identify red flags and anomalies.

2. **Legal Relevance**

   ➢ All findings must meet the standards of legal admissibility.

   ➢ Includes understanding legal concepts and working with attorneys.

3. **Analytical Precision**

   ➢ Relies on advanced analytical tools and methodologies to interpret data.

   ➢ Requires attention to detail and the ability to detect subtle discrepancies.

4. **Multidisciplinary Expertise**

   ➢ Combines accounting, auditing, law, psychology, and criminology knowledge.

   ➢ Involves skills like negotiation, interviewing, and cross-examination.

Difference Between Forensic Accounting and Traditional Accounting

Overview

Traditional accounting and forensic accounting share a common foundation in the principles of financial analysis, but their objectives, approaches, and applications diverge significantly. While conventional accounting focuses on accurately reporting and managing financial data, forensic accounting applies investigative techniques to uncover anomalies, fraud, and irregularities, often in legal or high-stakes contexts.

Key Differences

Aspect	Traditional Accounting	Forensic Accounting
Objective	The primary goal is to ensure accurate financial data recording, classification, and reporting for stakeholders such as management, investors, and regulatory authorities. It involves bookkeeping, preparation of financial statements, and compliance with tax laws.	This investigative discipline identifies fraud, financial misstatements, misconduct or irregularities. It often involves analysing data to provide evidence suitable for legal proceedings or disputes.
Approach	Transactional and procedural. Follows structured accounting principles, such as GAAP or IFRS. Relies on predefined processes, with minimal need for skepticism. Uses routine audits for assurance purposes.	Investigative and analytical. Involves a high degree of skepticism and scrutiny. Employs advanced data analysis techniques to trace irregularities. Adapts to unique circumstances, such as reconstructing destroyed financial records or tracing concealed transactions.
Primary Function	Prepares financial statements, budgets, reconciliations and tax returns.	Examines financial data for evidence of wrongdoing.
End Goal	Regulatory compliance and reporting.	Evidence gathering, collection and fraud detection/prevention.

Aspect	Traditional Accounting	Forensic Accounting
Tools Used	Manual registers, books, charts, etc. Accounting software, spreadsheets. Relies on standard accounting software like Tally, Zoho, QuickBooks, or SAP. Big corporations rely more on in-house developed software that fits their need.	Various advanced tools like IDEA, ACL, or Alteryx are used for data mining and analysis. It may involve techniques like Benford's Law for anomaly detection. Incorporates cyber-forensic tools to examine digital transactions and recover deleted files.
Stakeholders	Primarily serves the company's internal management, shareholders, Internal teams, regulators and auditors. Key outputs include financial statements, tax returns, and audit reports.	Caters to Management, legal teams, law enforcement, fraud detection units, and courts. Provides detailed investigative reports, expert opinions, and testimony.
Legal Relevance	Primarily focused on regulatory compliance and financial transparency. Rarely directly involved in legal cases unless financial statements are under dispute.	Findings are often part of legal investigations or court proceedings. Requires adherence to legal standards for evidence admissibility. The forensic accountant may act as an expert witness in court.
Scope of Work	Routine and standardised.	Complex and situation-specific investigations.
Time Frame	Ongoing, periodical (monthly, quarterly, annual).	Event-driven or based on incidents, often retrospective.

Aspect	Traditional Accounting	Forensic Accounting
Skill Set	Proficiency in accounting principles, tax laws, and financial analysis. Strong organisational and analytical skills.	A multidisciplinary approach requiring knowledge of accounting, auditing, law, criminology, and data analytics. Expertise in interviewing, negotiation, and investigative techniques.

Why Both Are Important??

Traditional accounting plays a vital role in ensuring that a company operates transparently and complies with legal and regulatory requirements, which helps maintain the confidence of stakeholders. On the other hand, forensic accounting is crucial when irregularities arise; it aids in resolving disputes, detecting fraud, and restoring financial integrity. Together, these two branches of accounting ensure the organisation's day-to-day financial health and effective crisis management.

Examples of Forensic Accounting in Action

1. Enron Scandal (2001): A Summary

The Enron scandal, one of the most infamous corporate frauds in history, led to the bankruptcy of Enron Corporation, a U.S. energy, commodities, and services company, and the dissolution of Arthur Andersen, one of the largest accounting firms at the time. It exposed systemic issues in corporate governance, accounting practices, and regulation.

Key Elements of the Scandal

1. Company Overview:

   ➢ Enron, headquartered in Houston, Texas, was established in 1985.

➢ It emerged as a market leader in energy trading and services, known for its innovation and rapid growth.

2. Fraudulent Activities:

➢ Off-Balance-Sheet Entities (Special Purpose Entities): Enron used complex financial structures to move debt and liabilities off its balance sheet, making the company appear more profitable.

➢ Mark-to-Market Accounting: Enron recognized projected profits from long-term contracts as current revenue, inflating its earnings.

3. Role of Arthur Andersen:

➢ As Enron's external auditor, Arthur Andersen failed to identify or report the fraudulent accounting practices.

➢ The firm also shredded documents during the investigation, which led to its criminal conviction for obstructing justice.

4. Revelation:

➢ In October 2001, Enron announced it was restating its earnings from 1997 to 2001 due to accounting irregularities.

➢ By December 2, 2001, Enron filed for bankruptcy, the largest in U.S. history.

Impact of the Scandal

1. Financial Consequences:

➢ Shareholders lost approximately $74 billion.

➢ Thousands of employees lost their jobs and retirement savings.

2. Regulatory Changes:

> ➤ The scandal led to the passage of the Sarbanes-Oxley Act (2002):
>
>> ▪ Established stricter rules for corporate governance and financial reporting.
>> ▪ Increased penalties for fraudulent financial activities.

3. Corporate and Public Lessons:

> ➤ Highlighted the need for transparency, ethical leadership, and robust internal controls.
> ➤ Exposed conflicts of interest between auditors and the companies they audited.

Significance

The Enron scandal remains a cautionary tale of unchecked corporate greed, ineffective oversight, and the devastating consequences of ethical lapses in financial management. It reshaped the regulatory and ethical landscape of corporate America.

2. Satyam Scandal (2009): A Summary

The Satyam scandal, often called "India's Enron," was a major corporate fraud that came to light in January 2009. It involved Satyam Computer Services Ltd., a leading IT services company based in India. The scandal exposed widespread financial manipulation, leading to significant reforms in India's corporate governance and auditing standards.

Key Elements of the Scandal

1. Company Overview:

> ➤ Satyam, headquartered in Hyderabad, was one of India's largest IT service providers, catering to global clients.
> ➤ Founded by Ramalinga Raju in 1987, the company was renowned for its rapid growth and innovation.

2. Fraudulent Activities:

> Falsification of Accounts:
> Satyam's founder, Ramalinga Raju, overstated the company's revenue, profits, and assets to present a rosy financial picture.

  - Fake cash reserves of ₹5,040 crore (approximately $1 billion) were reported.
  - Revenues were inflated through fake invoices.

> Corporate Malpractice:
> Funds were diverted to Raju's other ventures, including Maytas Infra and Maytas Properties, which his family owns.

3. Revelation:

> In January 2009, Ramalinga Raju admitted to the fraud in a letter to Satyam's board, stating, "It was like riding a tiger, not knowing how to get off without being eaten."
> The scandal wiped out shareholder wealth and sent shockwaves through India's corporate world.

Impact of the Scandal

1. Immediate Fallout:

> Satyam's shares plummeted by over 75% in a single day.
> The company faced delisting from global stock exchanges and loss of clients.
> Employees and stakeholders were left in turmoil.

2. Legal and Regulatory Repercussions:

> Ramalinga Raju and several executives were arrested and convicted of fraud, forgery, and breach of trust.
> The auditing firm PricewaterhouseCoopers (PwC), which failed to detect the fraud, faced heavy criticism and sanctions.

3. Acquisition and Revival:

    ➢ Satyam was eventually acquired by Tech Mahindra through a government-led bidding process in April 2009, ensuring the company's survival and saving thousands of jobs.

4. Regulatory Reforms:

    ➢ Strengthened corporate governance norms in India.
    ➢ It led to the establishment of tighter controls on auditors and stricter penalties for financial fraud.

Significance

The Satyam scandal was a wake-up call for corporate India. It highlighted vulnerabilities in governance, auditing, and regulatory frameworks and underscored the need for ethical leadership, transparent reporting, and vigilant oversight to prevent future fraud.

3. Punjab National Bank (PNB) Scam 2018: A Summary

The Punjab National Bank (PNB) scam, uncovered in early 2018, was one of the largest financial frauds in Indian history. The scam involved fraudulent transactions amounting to ₹11,400 crore (approximately $1.8 billion) and implicated prominent businessmen Nirav Modi and Mehul Choksi. It exposed serious lapses in banking operations, governance, and regulatory oversight.

Key Elements of the Scam

1. What Happened:

    ➢ The scam was orchestrated by Nirav Modi, a high-profile diamond merchant, and his co-owner, Mehul Choksi, owner of the Gitanjali Group.
    ➢ They used fraudulent Letters of Undertaking (LoUs) issued by PNB employees at a Mumbai branch to obtain foreign credit from overseas banks.

2. How the Scam Worked:

   ➢ PNB employees bypassed the bank's core banking system (CBS) to issue unauthorised LoUs.
   ➢ These LoUs were used to secure short-term loans from international branches of other Indian banks, with PNB acting as the guarantor.
   ➢ The loans were never repaid, leaving PNB liable for the entire amount.

3. Discovery:

   ➢ The scam came to light when PNB employees at the Brady House branch refused to issue fresh LoUs for Nirav Modi's companies without proper guarantees.
   ➢ An internal audit revealed the extent of the fraudulent activities spanning several years (2011–2018).

Impact of the Scam

1. Financial Fallout:

   ➢ PNB suffered massive financial losses, with its market valuation and investor confidence plummeting.
   ➢ The Reserve Bank of India (RBI) imposed stricter operational norms for issuing LoUs and Letters of Credit (LoCs), eventually banning their use.

2. Legal and Judicial Actions:

   ➢ Nirav Modi and Mehul Choksi fled India before the scam was uncovered, triggering an international manhunt.
   ➢ Nirav Modi was arrested in the UK in 2019 and is fighting extradition to India.
   ➢ Mehul Choksi fled to Antigua and is facing legal proceedings for extradition.

3. Government and Regulatory Reforms:

> ➢ Highlighted significant lapses in banking oversight and internal controls.
> ➢ The government introduced reforms to tighten fraud detection and strengthen bank accountability.
> ➢ Efforts were intensified to recover public money and punish those involved.

Significance

The PNB scam was a stark reminder of India's banking system vulnerabilities. It underscored the need for:

- Improved oversight in loan approvals and guarantee mechanisms.
- Robust internal controls to prevent abuse of the system.
- Greater accountability for both bank employees and regulators.

It prompted sweeping reforms in the financial sector and was a cautionary tale about unchecked power and systemic failures in corporate governance.

4. <u>Wirecard Scandal (2020): A Summary</u>

The Wirecard scandal was one of the biggest corporate frauds in European history. It led to the collapse of the German payment processor and financial services provider Wirecard AG. The scandal involved falsifying financial accounts totalling €1.9 billion (approximately $2.1 billion) and exposed severe regulatory failures in Germany's financial system.

Key Elements of the Scandal

1. Company Overview:

> ➢ Wirecard, founded in 1999, was a fintech pioneer offering electronic payment services, credit card issuing, and risk management.

> ➢ By 2018, it was listed on Germany's prestigious DAX 30 stock index, symbolising European success and innovation.

2. The Fraud:

   ➢ Wirecard claimed to have significant cash reserves, including €1.9 billion supposedly held in trustee accounts in the Philippines.

   ➢ Investigations revealed that these funds never existed, and Wirecard fabricated transactions to inflate revenues and profits.

3. Revelation:

   ➢ In June 2020, auditors from EY (Ernst & Young) refused to sign off on Wirecard's accounts, stating they couldn't confirm the existence of the €1.9 billion.

   ➢ CEO Markus Braun resigned and was later arrested. COO Jan Marsalek, a key figure in the scandal, fled and remains a fugitive.

Impact of the Scandal

1. Immediate Fallout:

   ➢ Wirecard filed for insolvency in June 2020, marking the first DAX 30-listed company to go bankrupt.

   ➢ Investors lost billions as the company's market valuation collapsed.

2. Regulatory Failures:

   ➢ Germany's financial watchdog, BaFin, faced heavy criticism for failing to act despite years of whistleblower warnings and investigative reports about irregularities.

   ➢ BaFin even targeted journalists who exposed the fraud, alleging they were manipulating the stock price.

3. Global Implications:

> ➢ Wirecard's operations impacted banks, payment processors, and businesses worldwide, with customers struggling to access funds and services.
> ➢ Major lenders and auditors faced scrutiny over their roles in enabling or overlooking the fraud.

Lessons and Reforms

1. Increased Oversight:

> ➢ The scandal called for stricter regulations for fintech companies and financial services.
> ➢ Germany implemented reforms to strengthen BaFin's independence and oversight powers.

2. Auditing Practices:

> ➢ EY faced lawsuits and a reputational hit for failing to detect the fraud despite years of auditing Wirecard.
> ➢ The case prompted reviews of global auditing standards and responsibilities.

3. Corporate Governance:

> ➢ Wirecard's failure highlighted weaknesses in corporate governance, including board accountability and checks on executive power.

Significance

The Wirecard scandal serves as a cautionary tale about the dangers of unchecked corporate power, regulatory complacency, and blind faith placed in rapidly growing companies. It also exposed vulnerabilities in the fintech sector and prompted global reforms to improve transparency, accountability, and oversight in financial services.

Importance of Forensic Accounting

1. **Mitigating Financial Crime**

   o Helps reduce economic losses caused by fraud, corruption, and financial misconduct.
   o Supports transparency and trust in financial systems.

2. **Assisting Legal Processes**

   o Provides courts with reliable and objective financial insights.
   o Strengthens the prosecution or defence in financial disputes.

3. **Ensuring Corporate Integrity**

   o Promotes adherence to ethical and regulatory standards.
   o Enhances stakeholder confidence in organisational governance.

4. **Adapting to Changing Dynamics**

   o With the rise of digital fraud and cryptocurrencies, forensic accounting adapts to new challenges, ensuring relevance in evolving landscapes.

Challenges in Forensic Accounting

1. **Complex Financial Schemes**: Sophisticated fraud schemes often involve layers of transactions that are difficult to trace.
2. **Lack of Standardised Practices**: Inconsistent practices across jurisdictions make forensic accounting challenging in global cases.
3. **Digital Evidence and Cybersecurity**: Handling and preserving digital evidence requires advanced technological expertise.
4. **Time and Cost Constraints"**: Investigations can be time-intensive and expensive, especially in large-scale cases.

Emerging Trends in Forensic Accounting

1. **Use of Artificial Intelligence (AI)**

    ➢ AI-driven tools to identify anomalies in large datasets.
    ➢ Machine learning algorithms for predictive fraud detection.

2. **Blockchain Technology**

    ➢ Enhances traceability and reduces fraud in transactions.
    ➢ Useful for tracking cryptocurrencies in financial crime investigations.

3. **Increased Regulatory Focus**

    ➢ Governments and regulatory bodies emphasise forensic accounting to combat corruption and enhance compliance.

4. **Integration with Cyber Forensics**

    ➢ Collaboration with IT experts to investigate cyber fraud and secure digital evidence.

Conclusion:

Forensic accounting goes beyond simple number crunching; it is a dynamic and investigative field that protects financial systems and ensures legal compliance. Its growing importance in addressing modern financial crimes makes forensic accounting an essential tool for businesses, governments, and legal systems. Forensic accounting plays a crucial role in today's complex business environment by providing the means to investigate and resolve financial issues that traditional accounting may not address. As companies face increasing risks of fraud and regulatory challenges, understanding the unique purposes and methods of forensic accounting is vital for safeguarding assets, maintaining compliance, and building trust in financial operations.

The following graph supports a strong narrative about **the rising importance and relevance** of forensic accounting as a profession, particularly in an era of **increasing financial complexity and digital fraud**.

Interpretation:

- The demand for forensic accounting has **tripled over the last decade**.
- This trend suggests growing recognition of forensic accountants as vital in:

    o Detecting and preventing fraud,
    o Supporting litigation,
    o Ensuring financial transparency and compliance.

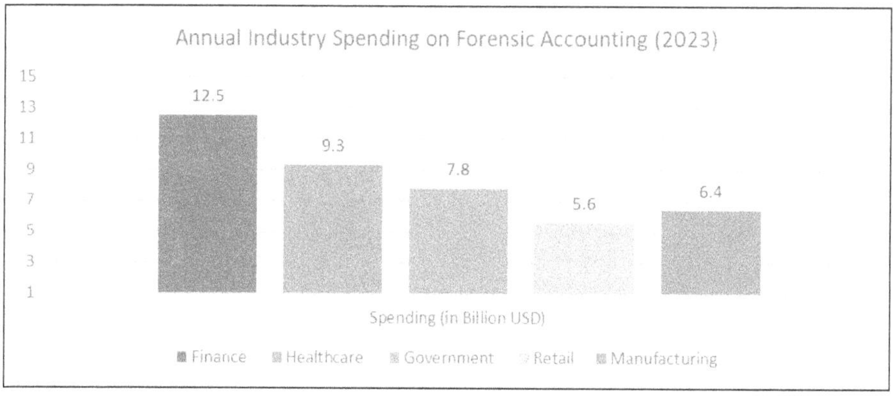

The **"Annual Industry Spending on Forensic Accounting (2023)"** graph illustrates how different sectors invest in forensic accounting services. Here's a simple summary:

Insights:

- Finance leads all sectors, spending $12.5 billion, which reflects its significant exposure to fraud risk and regulatory scrutiny.
- Healthcare follows, with substantial spending due to billing, insurance, and compliance fraud.
- The government allocates considerable funds for public accountability and anti-corruption Initiatives.

- Retail and Manufacturing invest less but still allocate resources toward fraud detection and supply chain monitoring.

This chart underscores the sector-specific reliance on forensic accounting, highlighting where forensic professionals are most needed. You could use this to discuss targeted career paths or service opportunities for forensic experts in high-spending sectors.

Chapter 02

Key Principles of Forensic Accounting

"Ethics as a Competitive Advantage"

Introduction to Ethics in Forensic Accounting

Ethics are the foundation of forensic accounting, ensuring integrity, objectivity, and trust within the profession. Unlike traditional accountants, forensic accountants often operate in high-stakes environments, such as fraud investigations and litigation support, where ethical dilemmas frequently arise. Upholding high ethical standards is crucial for preserving the credibility and integrity of the process.

In forensic accounting, the accountant's role extends beyond uncovering the truth; they must also maintain integrity and impartiality. Forensic accountants handle sensitive financial data and must adhere to the highest ethical standards to ensure credibility and objectivity in their investigations.

Core Ethical Principles in Forensic Accounting

1. **Integrity**

   ➢ Forensic accountants must adhere to honesty and moral principles, even when faced with pressure from clients or stakeholders.

   ➢ Examples:

      ▪ Refusing to alter findings to favour a client during litigation.

      ▪ Disclosing potential conflicts of interest that might compromise objectivity.

2. **Objectivity and Independence**

   ➢ Accountants must remain impartial and unbiased in their investigations and analyses.
   ➢ Scenarios where objectivity might be tested:

   - Pressure from management to overlook irregularities.
   - Personal relationships with individuals being investigated.

   ➢ Safeguards:

   - Establishing clear boundaries with stakeholders.
   - Using third-party reviews to ensure findings remain unbiased.

3. **Confidentiality**

   ➢ Safeguarding sensitive information obtained during investigations is paramount.
   ➢ Ethical dilemmas in confidentiality:

   - Balancing the need to protect client information with legal requirements to disclose findings in court.
   - Avoiding unauthorised sharing of proprietary data.

   ➢ Best practices:

   - Signing non-disclosure agreements (NDAs).
   - Storing data securely using encrypted systems.

4. **Professional Competence**

   ➢ Forensic accountants must continuously update their skills to remain effective, especially given the rise of digital fraud and emerging technologies.
   ➢ Ethical obligation:

   - Avoiding tasks beyond one's expertise or qualifications.

➢ Example:

- Referring cases involving advanced cybersecurity breaches to specialists rather than attempting to handle them independently.

5. **Due Care**

➢ Forensic accountants must exercise diligence and care in their work, avoiding negligence.
➢ This includes:

- Thoroughly verifying evidence.
- Avoiding premature conclusions.

➢ Real-world impact:

- A poorly conducted investigation could harm an innocent party's reputation or let fraudsters evade justice.

6. **Transparency and Accountability**

➢ Ethical forensic accountants must clearly and accurately explain their findings, methodologies, and limitations.
➢ Ensuring accountability through documentation:

- Maintaining an audit trail of decisions and actions taken during investigations.
- Properly citing sources and disclosing assumptions in reports.

Common Ethical Challenges in Forensic Accounting

1. **Conflict of Interest**

➢ Dilemma: Investigating a company while maintaining a financial or personal relationship with its executives.
➢ Ethical resolution: Recusal or disclosure of potential conflicts to uphold integrity.

2. **Pressure from Stakeholders**

> ➢ Dilemma: A client requests to downplay findings or exclude damaging evidence.
>
> ➢ Ethical resolution: Adhering to professional standards and refusing to alter facts.

3. **Whistleblowing**

> ➢ Dilemma: Identifying fraud within a client organisation while encountering resistance to disclose findings.
>
> ➢ Ethical resolution: Adhering to whistleblower laws or reporting to the appropriate authorities while safeguarding the whistleblower's identity.

4. **Cultural and Legal Differences**

> ➢ Dilemma: Working in a country where bribery is common practice, conflicting with international ethical standards.
>
> ➢ Ethical resolution: Complying with universal principles like the *Code of Ethics for Professional Accountants* by IFAC, even when local norms differ.

Ethical Frameworks and Guidelines

1. **Professional Codes of Conduct**

> ➢ International Federation of Accountants (IFAC) Code of Ethics for Professional Accountants: A global standard for ethical behaviour.
>
> ➢ Guidelines from national accounting bodies such as ICAI (India), AICPA (USA), and others.

2. **Legal Frameworks**

> ➢ Anti-fraud laws, such as the Sarbanes-Oxley Act in the USA, emphasise ethical reporting and auditing practices.

> Case Example: SOX requirements for whistleblower protections foster ethical behaviour in forensic investigations.

3. Ethics Training and Certification

> Many certifications (e.g., CFE, CPA) include ethical guidelines to help professionals navigate dilemmas.

Real-Life Examples of Ethical Failures

1. Case Study: Arthur Andersen and Enron

> Ethical lapse: The audit firm compromised its independence by helping Enron conceal financial misconduct.

> Result: The firm's downfall and loss of public trust in the auditing profession.

2. Case Study: WorldCom Fraud

> Ethical lapse: Internal auditors failed to report financial discrepancies, enabling continued fraud.

> Result: Bankruptcy and regulatory overhauls.

Strategies to Maintain High Ethical Standards

1. Institutional Safeguards

> Implementing ethics committees within organisations.

> Encouraging anonymous reporting channels for employees to highlight unethical practices.

2. Personal Accountability

> Forensic accountants must hold themselves accountable to ethical principles, even in adverse circumstances.

3. Adopting Technology

> Use AI-powered tools to remove human biases in fraud detection and ensure data accuracy.

Key Takeaways for Readers

- Ethical conduct isn't just a professional obligation; it's essential for ensuring the credibility and sustainability of forensic accounting practices.
- Businesses must prioritise ethics as part of their governance framework to minimise fraud and protect their reputation.
- Forensic accountants play a critical role as guardians of financial integrity, and their ethical choices can profoundly impact individuals, companies, and society.

Ethical Code Checklist for Forensic Accountants

Integrity

- Have I been honest and transparent in my actions and decisions?
- Have I avoided misleading or misrepresenting any facts?
- Am I willing to stand by my findings, even if they are unfavourable to stakeholders?

Objectivity and Independence

- Have I maintained impartiality throughout the investigation?
- Have I identified and disclosed any potential conflicts of interest?
- Have I avoided undue influence from clients, management, or other parties?

Confidentiality

- Have I protected all sensitive information obtained during the investigation?
- Have I shared data only with authorised individuals or as required by law?
- Have I implemented measures to secure data storage and transmission?

Professional Competence and Due Care

- Have I worked within the boundaries of my expertise?
- Have I conducted thorough analyses, leaving no stone unturned?
- Have I kept up-to-date with the latest tools, technologies, and regulations?

Transparency and Accountability

- Have I documented all processes, findings, and assumptions?
- Have I provided detailed and unbiased explanations of my conclusions?
- Have I ensured that my work is traceable and can withstand scrutiny?

General Ethical Practices

- Am I adhering to my profession's code of conduct (e.g., IFAC, ICAI, AICPA)?
- Have I upheld the principles of fairness and justice in my work?
- Have I considered the broader impact of my findings on stakeholders and society?

Actions to Take in Case of Ethical Dilemmas

- Consult professional ethical guidelines and legal standards.
- Seek advice from peers, mentors, or ethics committees.
- Escalate unresolved issues to appropriate authorities or legal counsel.

Key Ethical Guidelines Summary

1. Always act in the public interest, not just the client's interest.
2. Do not compromise on truth, even under pressure.
3. Document and justify every action and decision with evidence.
4. Stay vigilant to ensure independence and objectivity at all times.
5. Commit to continuous learning and self-regulation to adapt to evolving challenges.

The "Ethical Standards vs Financial Health" graph shows a positive correlation between a company's ethical score and financial health score. Here's a simple summary:

Key Insights:

- As ethical scores increase, financial health scores improve as well.
- Companies with low ethical standards (e.g., a score of 41) generally exhibit lower financial health (with a score around 45).
- Conversely, companies with high ethical standards (e.g., score 100) typically enjoy stronger financial health (score around 120).

Interpretation:

- This indicates that ethical behaviour is linked to financial well-being.
- Ethical companies may excel at managing risk, building stakeholder trust, and avoiding costly legal or reputational issues, resulting in improved financial outcomes.

Why This Matters in Forensic Accounting:

- Forensic accountants can use ethical benchmarking to predict financial vulnerabilities or fraud risks.
- Promoting higher ethical standards may serve as a preventive control against financial misconduct.

The "Compliance Rates with Forensic Standards by Region" chart illustrates how effectively different regions adhere to forensic accounting standards:

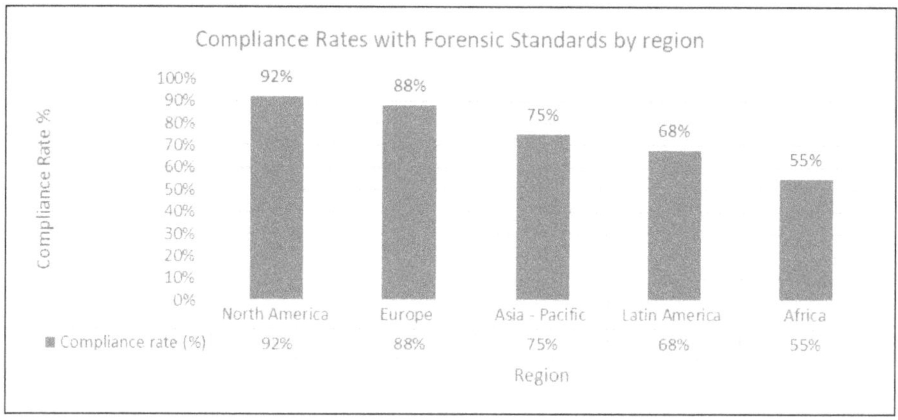

This graph emphasises the global disparities in forensic readiness and the adoption of these standards. Here's a summary:

Key Insights:

- North America and Europe display the highest compliance levels, likely due to stronger regulatory frameworks and established forensic practices.
- Asia-Pacific and Latin America exhibit moderate compliance, indicating evolving standards and practices.
- Africa has the lowest compliance rate, potentially due to limited resources, training, or enforcement mechanisms.

Introduction to the Legal Framework for Forensic Accounting

Forensic accounting in India functions within a clearly defined legal and regulatory framework. Strong understanding of the relevant laws, guidelines, and standards is essential for forensic accountants. This knowledge ensures compliance, accountability, and the admissibility of their findings in legal proceedings.

Key Laws Governing Forensic Accounting in India

1. Bharatiya Nyaya Sanhita (BNS), 2023

India's new criminal code replaces the colonial-era Indian Penal Code (IPC) of 1860. Parliament enacted it in December 2023, and it came into force on July 1, 2024. The BNS aims to modernise India's criminal justice system by incorporating contemporary legal standards, technological advancements, and a focus on victim-centric justice. Which replaces the Indian Penal Code (IPC), the provisions addressing financial crimes have been restructured as follows:

A. Dishonest Misappropriation of Property:

Section 312 pertains to the dishonest misappropriation or conversion of movable property for one's own use, aligning with the former Section 403 of the IPC.

B. Criminal Breach of Trust:

Section 314 deals with instances where an individual entrusted with property dishonestly misappropriates or converts it, corresponding to the previous Section 406 of the IPC.

C. Cheating and Dishonestly Inducing Delivery of Property:

Section 316: This section addresses the act of cheating and dishonestly inducing another person to deliver property, similar to the erstwhile Section 420 of the IPC.

2. The Companies Act, 2013

- ➤ Sections relevant to fraud:

    - Section 447: Punishment for fraud.
    - Section 248: Removal of company name if involved in fraud or unlawful activities.

- ➤ Role of forensic accountants:

    - Investigating discrepancies in company financials during audits or disputes.
    - Reporting fraud to authorities as mandated by Section 143(12).

3. The Prevention of Money Laundering Act (PMLA), 2002

- ➤ Overview:

    - Addresses money laundering and empowers authorities to trace and attach properties obtained through criminal activities.

- ➤ Role of forensic accountants:

    - Identifying suspicious transactions and assisting in tracing laundered funds.
    - Preparing reports for submission to the Financial Intelligence Unit – India (FIU-IND).

4. The Information Technology Act, 2000

- ➤ Key sections for digital fraud:

    - Section 66C: Identity theft.
    - Section 66D: Cheating by personation using computer resources.
    - Section 72A: Punishment for disclosure of information in breach of a lawful contract.

- ➤ Role in forensic investigations:

  - Collecting and preserving digital evidence, such as emails, transaction logs, and metadata.

5. The Income Tax Act, 1961

- ➤ Relevant provisions:

  - Sections dealing with tax evasion and fraudulent claims.

- ➤ Forensic accountants assist in identifying:

  - Tax evasion practices, such as underreporting income or inflating expenses.
  - Misuse of deductions or exemptions.

6. The Insolvency and Bankruptcy Code (IBC), 2016

- ➤ Importance:

  - Provides a legal framework for resolving insolvency and bankruptcy cases.

- ➤ Role of forensic accountants:

  - Investigating financial irregularities in insolvent companies.
  - Assisting resolution professionals in identifying fraudulent transactions.

7. The SEBI Act, 1992

- ➤ Importance:

  - Regulates securities markets and addresses fraudulent practices in trading and IPOs.

- ➤ Forensic accountants assist SEBI by:

  - Investigating insider trading, stock manipulation, and corporate governance failures.

Understanding these provisions helps identify elements of financial fraud, which can aid in investigation and reporting.

Regulatory Bodies Relevant to Forensic Accounting in India

1. **Institute of Chartered Accountants of India (ICAI)**

    o Ethical standards and guidelines:

      - ICAI Code of Ethics: Defines the ethical responsibilities of chartered accountants, including forensic accountants.
      - Guidance on reporting financial fraud and compliance with anti-fraud laws.

2. **Reserve Bank of India (RBI)**

    o Role in forensic investigations:

      - Mandates the reporting of suspicious financial transactions by banks.
      - Implements frameworks for detecting financial fraud in the banking sector.

3. **Serious Fraud Investigation Office (SFIO)**

    o Functions:

      - Investigates major corporate frauds.
      - Role of forensic accountants:
      - Assisting in gathering and analysing financial evidence for SFIO investigations.

4. **Financial Intelligence Unit – India (FIU-IND)**

    o Role:

      - Monitors and analyses financial transactions for anti-money laundering compliance.

- o Contribution of forensic accountants:

  - Identifying suspicious activity reports (SARs) for submission to FIU-IND.

Standards and Frameworks for Forensic Accounting in India

1. **Accounting and Auditing Standards**

   - ➢ Indian Accounting Standards (Ind AS) and Standards on Auditing (SAs):

     - Forensic accountants must ensure their work aligns with these standards to maintain investigation accuracy and reliability.

2. **Forensic Accounting Standards**

   - ➢ Lack of dedicated forensic accounting standards in India:

     - However, global frameworks like those by the *Association of Certified Fraud Examiners* (ACFE) can provide guidance.

3. **Evidence Collection and Admissibility Standards**

   - ➢ **Bharatiya Sakshya Adhiniyam (BSA), 2023** is a comprehensive legislative reform enacted to modernise and replace the colonial-era Indian Evidence Act (IEA) of 1872. This new law aims to align India's evidence framework with contemporary technological advancements and societal needs.

     - Specifies the requirements for presenting evidence in court.
     - Forensic accountants must ensure proper collection, preservation, and chain of custody for evidence to be admissible.

Case Studies to Illustrate Legal Framework in Action

1. **Satyam Scandal (2009)**

   ➢ Legal implications:

     ▪ Violation of the Companies Act and Bharatiya Nyaya Sanhita (BNS), 2023 (IPC) sections related to forgery and misappropriation.

   ➢ Forensic accounting role:

     ▪ Uncovering falsified revenues, inflated profits, and irregularities in fixed deposits.

2. **Punjab National Bank (PNB) Scam (2018)**

   ➢ Legal focus:

     ▪ Fraudulent issuance of Letters of Undertaking under the Bharatiya Nyaya Sanhita (BNS), 2023 (IPC) and PMLA.

   ➢ Forensic accounting role:

     ▪ Tracing the misuse of funds and linking it to perpetrators.

3. **DHFL Scam (2019)**

   ➢ Legal breaches:

     ▪ Violations under the Companies Act, PMLA, and IT Act.

   ➢ Forensic accounting role:

     ▪ Identifying shell companies and tracing diverted funds.

Key Takeaways for Forensic Accountants in India

1. **Knowledge of Indian Laws:**

   ➢ A deep understanding of the IPC, Companies Act, and other laws is essential for effective investigation.

2. **Collaboration with Regulators**:

   ➢ Building working relationships with SFIO, SEBI, and RBI ensures smoother investigations.

3. **Digital Expertise**:

   ➢ Familiarity with IT Act provisions is critical for addressing cybercrime and digital fraud.

4. **Focus on Evidence Admissibility**:

   ➢ Adherence to the Bharatiya Sakshya Adhiniyam (BSA), 2023 (formerly Indian Evidence Act) safeguards the credibility of forensic reports in court.

Practical Tips and Tools for Navigating Legal Frameworks in Forensic Accounting

To ensure compliance and efficiency in navigating India's legal frameworks, forensic accountants can adopt the following strategies and tools:

Practical Tips for Forensic Accountants

1. **Stay Updated on Laws and Regulations**

   ➢ Regularly review amendments to laws like the Companies Act, PMLA, and IT Act.
   ➢ Follow updates from regulatory bodies such as ICAI, SEBI, and RBI.
   ➢ Participate in webinars, workshops, and certification programs on forensic accounting.

2. **Adopt a Proactive Approach to Compliance**

   ➢ Familiarise yourself with the penalties and consequences of non-compliance.

> Establish a checklist of applicable laws for each case to ensure thoroughness.
> Seek guidance from legal counsel when dealing with complex cases.

3. Prioritise Evidence Handling

> Maintain a clear chain of custody for physical and digital evidence.
> Use secure storage systems for sensitive data to prevent unauthorised access.
> Understand admissibility standards under the Bharatiya Sakshya Adhiniyam (BSA), 2023 (formerly Indian Evidence Act) to prepare robust cases.

4. Collaborate with Legal and Regulatory Experts

> Work closely with legal advisors and auditors to interpret complex legal provisions.
> Consult with law enforcement agencies, such as the Enforcement Directorate (ED) or SFIO, when necessary.
> Build relationships with compliance officers in banks and corporations to identify fraud early.

5. Incorporate Technological Solutions

> Use software tools to enhance data analysis, evidence collection, and reporting efficiency.
> Leverage AI for fraud detection and blockchain technology for traceability in financial transactions.

6. Develop Clear and Defensible Reports

> Document all findings systematically, referencing applicable legal provisions.
> Ensure reports are factual, unbiased, and free from ambiguity to withstand scrutiny in legal proceedings.

Recommended Tools and Technologies

1. **Data Analytics Tools**

   - **ACL Analytics** and **CaseWare IDEA**: Useful for identifying anomalies and patterns in financial data.
   - **Microsoft Power BI** and **Tableau**: For creating dynamic visualisations that communicate findings effectively.

2. **Digital Forensics Software**

   - **EnCase Forensic** and **FTK (Forensic Toolkit)**: For examining digital evidence like emails, logs, and documents.
   - **X-Ways Forensics**: A cost-effective solution for data recovery and analysis.

3. **Fraud Detection Tools**

   - **SAS Fraud Management**: This is used to monitor and detect fraud in banking and financial institutions.
   - **Actimize**: To prevent financial crime and comply with anti-money laundering regulations.

4. **Document Management and Evidence Collection**

   - **DocuSign**: To manage and authenticate legal documents.
   - **Chainkit**: To ensure a tamper-proof chain of custody for digital evidence.

5. **AI and Machine Learning Tools**

   - **FraudLens:** Uses AI to identify fraud patterns in large datasets.
   - **H2O.ai:** An open-source AI platform for advanced analytics and fraud detection.

Example Workflow for Navigating Legal Frameworks

1. **Initial Assessment**

   - Review case details to identify relevant legal provisions (e.g., IPC, PMLA).

- Gather initial data and evaluate its compliance with laws.

2. **Data Collection and Analysis**

   - Use analytics tools to examine financial transactions for irregularities.
   - Apply digital forensics techniques to collect and secure evidence.

3. **Legal Collaboration**

   - Discuss findings with legal teams to validate interpretations of laws.
   - Align investigation goals with legal requirements for prosecution.

4. **Report Preparation**

   - Reference legal frameworks in reports to substantiate findings.
   - Include actionable recommendations for legal and regulatory compliance.

5. **Presentation in Legal Settings**

   - Prepare concise summaries of evidence and align them with case laws.
   - Practice delivering expert testimony to explain findings effectively in court.

Key Takeaway for Practical Application

Forensic accountants leverage their deep understanding of India's legal system alongside modern tools to conduct thorough and legally sound investigations.

Ethics and legal standards are essential in forensic accounting. By adhering to these principles, forensic accountants can perform their duties responsibly and professionally. This commitment ensures their findings are accurate, objective, and compliant with the law. With this strong foundation, they effectively support investigations, safeguard assets, and uphold the integrity of financial reporting and business operations.

Chapter 03

The Role of a Forensic Accountant

"The Financial Detective: Skills and Mindset of Today's Forensic Accountant"

Skills and Qualifications Required

Forensic accountants are highly specialised professionals who combine traditional accounting knowledge with strong investigative and analytical skills. Their work is essential in identifying financial discrepancies, preventing fraudulent activities, and advancing legal investigations. This multifaceted role requires a unique blend of technical expertise, meticulous analytical abilities, and effective interpersonal skills. Forensic accountants are equipped to detect, prevent, and investigate financial crimes and ethical violations.

The complexity of this profession demands a distinctive combination of skills that sets forensic accountants apart. Their ability to unravel intricate financial stories requires analytical rigour and the capability to communicate findings clearly and effectively. This chapter will examine the essential skills and qualifications that enable these professionals to succeed in this dynamic and impactful field.

1. **Core Skills Required for a Forensic Accountant**

a. Analytical and Critical Thinking Skills

- **Why Important:**
  Forensic accountants must examine complex financial data and identify inconsistencies or patterns indicative of fraud.

- **Example:**
  Spotting anomalies in expense accounts or tracing irregular transactions in a corporate audit.

- **Skills:**
  - ➢ Logical reasoning.
  - ➢ Ability to connect disparate pieces of information.
  - ➢ Aptitude for solving complex problems.

b. Financial and Accounting Expertise

- **Why Important:**
  Strong knowledge of accounting principles and financial regulations is essential for understanding and analysing data.

- **Skills:**
  - ➢ Mastery of GAAP (Generally Accepted Accounting Principles) and IFRS (International Financial Reporting Standards).
  - ➢ Proficiency in auditing standards.
  - ➢ Understanding taxation laws and compliance requirements.

c. Investigative and Research Skills

- **Why Important:**
  Forensic accountants must often trace hidden assets, investigate fraudulent schemes, and rebuild financial records.

- **Skills:**
  - ➢ Conducting thorough background research.
  - ➢ Utilising forensic tools for financial analysis.
  - ➢ Ability to reconstruct data from incomplete or destroyed records.

d. Knowledge of Legal Framework

- **Why Important:**
  Forensic accounting findings are often used in court cases, requiring an understanding of legal standards and evidence rules.

- **Skills:**
  - ➤ Awareness of Indian laws, such as the Indian Penal Code, Companies Act, and Evidence Act.
  - ➤ Familiarity with international anti-fraud laws, such as the Foreign Corrupt Practices Act (FCPA).
  - ➤ Knowledge of evidence documentation and admissibility in court.

e. Technological Proficiency

- **Why Important:**
  Modern forensic accounting relies heavily on technology to analyse data and detect patterns.

- **Skills:**
  - ➤ Proficiency in forensic tools like ACL, IDEA, or CaseWare.
  - ➤ Expertise in data visualisation platforms like Tableau or Power BI.
  - ➤ Familiarity with cyber forensics and blockchain technology to track digital assets and cryptocurrencies.

f. Communication and Presentation Skills

- **Why Important:**
  A forensic accountant must present findings clearly to stakeholders, including management, lawyers, and courts.

- **Skills:**
  - ➤ Report writing that is concise, factual, and legally sound.
  - ➤ Delivering expert testimony in a way that is easy to understand.
  - ➤ Collaborating effectively with legal teams and law enforcement.

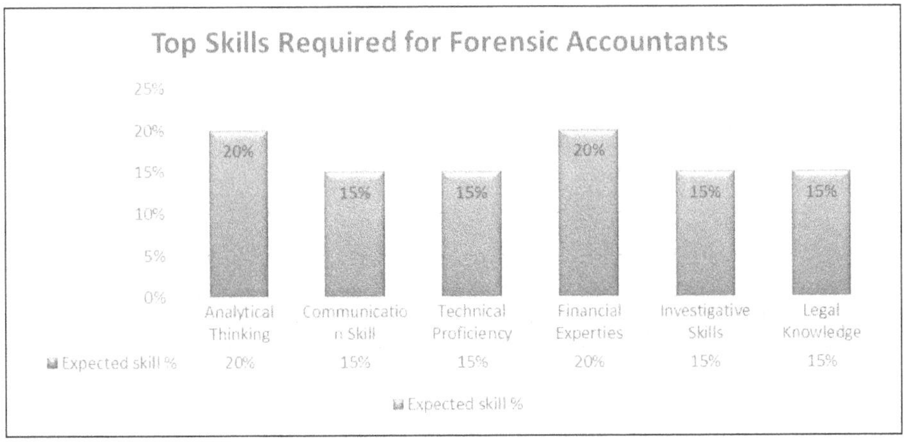

2. Qualifications and Certifications

a. Educational Background

- A bachelor's degree in accounting, finance, or a related field is typically required.
- A Master's degree in forensic accounting, financial crime investigation, or business law can provide an edge.

b. Professional Certifications

- **Chartered Accountant (CA):**
  Provides foundational knowledge in accounting and auditing.

- **Certified Fraud Examiner (CFE):**
  Focuses on fraud detection and prevention.

- **Certified Forensic Accounting Professional (CFAP):**
  Specific to forensic accounting practices in India.

- **Certified Public Accountant (CPA):**
  Internationally recognised certification for accounting professionals.

- **Certified Anti-Money Laundering Specialist (CAMS):**
  Specialising in combating money laundering and financial crimes.

c. Continuing Education

- Forensic accountants must stay updated on evolving fraud tactics, regulatory changes, and technological advancements.
- Regular participation in workshops, seminars, and online courses is essential.

3. Additional Attributes for Success

a. Scepticism

- A questioning mindset is critical for uncovering concealed fraud.

b. Integrity and Ethical Standards

- Forensic accountants must uphold high ethical standards as their findings influence legal and financial decisions.

c. Attention to Detail

- Meticulousness is key to identifying subtle irregularities or overlooked evidence.

d. Time Management and Stress Handling

- Forensic investigations often involve tight deadlines and high stakes.

4. Real-World Applications of Skills

- **Case Study 1:**
  A forensic accountant traced hidden assets during a high-profile divorce case, uncovering offshore accounts.

- **Case Study 2:**
  During a corporate embezzlement investigation, an accountant used forensic software to identify unauthorised transactions disguised as legitimate expenses.

Responsibilities and Typical Day-to-Day Activities

Forensic accountants are highly specialised professionals who play a crucial role in uncovering financial misconduct and ensuring adherence to legal regulations. Their work primarily involves investigating complex financial transactions to identify irregularities, detect potential fraud, and provide expert testimony in legal proceedings. Unlike conventional accountants, forensic accountants must excel not only in technical accounting skills but also in investigative techniques.

On a day-to-day basis, their responsibilities include examining financial records, analysing data trends, and employing forensic technology to trace illicit activities. They often collaborate with law enforcement agencies, legal teams, and regulatory bodies, providing insights that can lead to prosecuting fraudulent acts. Moreover, forensic accountants are adept at preparing detailed reports that clearly articulate their findings, which may be used in court cases.

In summary, the day-to-day work of forensic accountants is a blend of meticulous data analysis, legal consultation, and investigative detective work, making them invaluable in the fight against financial crime and in upholding the integrity of financial systems.

1. **Key Responsibilities of a Forensic Accountant**

a. Investigating Financial Irregularities

- **Objective:**
  Identify and analyse discrepancies in financial statements, records, or transactions.

- **Activities:**
  - Tracing unauthorised transactions in corporate accounts.
  - Examining discrepancies in payroll or expense reports.
  - Detecting patterns that suggest fraud or embezzlement.

- **Example:**
  Uncovering a multi-layered scheme of kickbacks in vendor payments.

b. Fraud Detection and Prevention

- **Objective:**
  Proactively implement systems to prevent fraud before it occurs.

- **Activities:**
  - ➢ Designing and reviewing internal control systems.
  - ➢ Conducting fraud risk assessments across departments.
  - ➢ Educating employees on ethical practices and fraud red flags.

- **Example:**
  Developing a whistleblower policy that empowers employees to report unethical activities anonymously.

c. Legal Support and Evidence Preparation

- **Objective:**
  Provide litigation support by collecting and analysing financial evidence for legal proceedings.

- **Activities:**
  - ➢ Collaborating with legal teams to prepare cases.
  - ➢ Documenting findings in legally admissible formats.
  - ➢ Serving as expert witnesses during trials.

- **Example:**
  Presenting financial evidence in court to demonstrate the flow of funds in a money laundering case.

d. Asset Tracing and Recovery

- **Objective:**
  Locate and recover stolen or hidden assets during financial disputes or fraud investigations.

- **Activities:**
  - ➢ Tracing the movement of funds through multiple bank accounts.
  - ➢ Identifying offshore investments or hidden properties.
  - ➢ Assisting law enforcement agencies in asset recovery operations.

- **Example:**
  Locating undisclosed overseas properties in a corporate fraud investigation.

e. Compliance and Regulatory Oversight

- **Objective:**
  Ensure businesses comply with financial laws and regulations.

- **Activities:**
  - ➢ Conducting compliance audits.
  - ➢ Advising on anti-money laundering (AML) and Know Your Customer (KYC) policies.
  - ➢ Monitoring adherence to taxation laws and corporate governance standards.

- **Example:**
  Helping a multinational company implement stricter AML controls to avoid regulatory penalties.

f. Educating and Training Stakeholders

- **Objective:**
  Raise awareness and strengthen the organisation's ability to detect and prevent fraud.

- **Activities:**
  - ➢ Training employees on fraud detection techniques.
  - ➢ Conducting workshops for senior management on internal controls.

> ➢ Sharing case studies and best practices in forensic accounting.

- **Example:**
  Leading a workshop on detecting invoice fraud for finance teams.

2. Typical Day-to-Day Activities of a Forensic Accountant

a. Morning Routine: Reviewing and Analysing Data

- Begin the day by reviewing the latest financial data, reports, or case updates.
- Analyse anomalies flagged by automated tools or previous investigations.
- Prioritise tasks based on deadlines or ongoing cases.

b. Midday Tasks: Investigations and Collaboration

- Conduct interviews with employees or stakeholders to gather evidence.
- Meet with legal teams, auditors, or management to discuss findings.
- Use forensic tools to trace transactions or reconstruct financial records.
- Document progress and findings in detailed reports.

c. Afternoon: Technology and Reporting

- Leverage forensic software to analyse large datasets or detect patterns.
- Prepare presentations or reports summarising key findings.
- Design recommendations for strengthening internal controls.

d. Ad-Hoc Tasks:

- Respond to urgent fraud alerts or crises.
- Provide real-time advice to legal teams during hearings.
- Collaborate with law enforcement agencies during on-site investigations.

3. Unique Challenges in Their Responsibilities

- **Handling Complex Cases:**
  Multi-jurisdictional fraud cases involving international regulations.

- **Maintaining Confidentiality:**
  Sensitive investigations require discretion to protect whistleblowers or company reputations.

- **Working Under Pressure:**
  Tight deadlines and high-stakes cases demand focus and resilience.

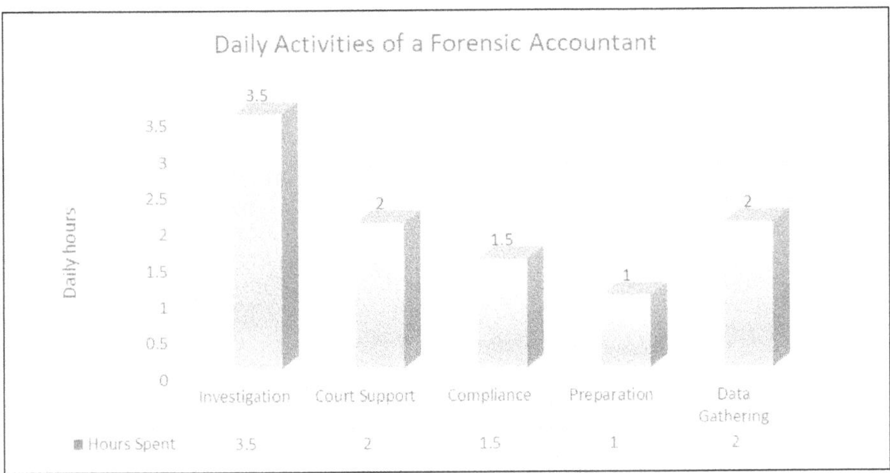

Conclusion:

The role of a forensic accountant is diverse and challenging, requiring a combination of financial expertise, investigative skills, and ethical integrity. Forensic accountants play a crucial role in examining daily transactions, providing expert testimony in court, and helping businesses protect their assets, maintain compliance, and uphold financial integrity. Understanding their skills, qualifications, and responsibilities is important for anyone considering a career in this field or seeking the services of a forensic accountant.

Part 2

Techniques and Tools in Forensic Accounting

Chapter 04

Investigative Techniques

"Unmasking the Hidden Truths in Financial Data"

Data Collection and Analysis

Data collection and analysis are essential components of forensic accounting. Gathering relevant financial information is crucial for uncovering fraud, misappropriation, or other irregularities. Effective forensic accounting investigations start with thorough data collection. Forensic accountants gather data from various sources, ensuring it is reliable and legally admissible in court. These data collection techniques allow forensic accountants to identify irregularities, detect fraudulent activities, and gather evidence to support legal proceedings.

This chapter focuses on how data is collected, analysed, and interpreted in the context of forensic accounting investigations.

1. Data Collection in Forensic Accounting

a. Sources of Data

Forensic accountants rely on multiple sources for collecting data, including:

1. **Internal Sources:**

   - **Financial Statements:** Balance sheets, profit and loss statements, cash flow statements.
   - **Invoices and Receipts:** These are used to trace the authenticity of transactions.

> **Employee Records:** Payroll data, expense claims, and attendance records.

> **Email and Communication Logs:** For evidence of collusion or misconduct.

2. **External Sources:**

> **Bank Statements:** These are used to identify unauthorised withdrawals or deposits.

> **Third-Party Records:** Vendor invoices, contracts, and agreements.

> **Regulatory Filings:** Tax records, company registration documents, and compliance reports.

> **Public Data:** Court filings, news reports, or online public databases.

b. Methods of Data Collection

1. **Document Review:**

> Examining paper and electronic records for completeness, accuracy, and authenticity.

2. **Interviews and Questionnaires:**

> Gathering information from employees, management, and third parties.

3. **Digital Forensics:**

> Extracting and recovering data from hard drives, email servers, and cloud storage.

4. **Observation:**

> Monitoring workplace activities to identify discrepancies in operations or procedures.

5. **Whistleblower Reports:**

> ➤ Reviewing tips or anonymous complaints as a starting point for investigations.

2. Data Analysis in Forensic Accounting

a. Objectives of Data Analysis

- **Identify Patterns:** Highlight unusual trends in financial transactions.
- **Detect Anomalies:** Spot deviations from expected behaviour, such as inflated invoices or unauthorised expenses.
- **Corroborate Evidence:** Cross-verify data across multiple sources to ensure consistency.
- **Generate Insights:** Provide actionable recommendations for mitigating risks or pursuing legal action.

b. Techniques for Data Analysis

1. **Trend Analysis:**

> ➤ Comparing historical data to identify irregular patterns.
> ➤ Example: A sudden spike in vendor payments without corresponding invoices.

2. **Ratio Analysis:**

> ➤ Calculating financial ratios (e.g., debt-to-equity, gross profit margin) to uncover inconsistencies.
> ➤ Example: An unusually high accounts receivable turnover might indicate fake sales.

3. **Benford's Law Analysis:**

> ➤ Using statistical principles to detect fabricated numbers in financial data.
> ➤ Example: Fake invoices often fail to follow the natural distribution of digits.

4. **Data Mining:**

    ➢ Leveraging software to identify correlations and outliers in large datasets.

    ➢ Example: Detecting a pattern of payments to shell companies.

5. **Network Analysis:**

    ➢ Mapping relationships between entities to expose fraudulent connections.

    ➢ Example: Identifying links between employees and suspicious vendors.

c. Tools for Data Analysis

1. **Excel and Spreadsheet Tools:**

    ➢ Performing basic analysis and calculations.

2. **Forensic Accounting Software:**

    ➢ Specialised tools like IDEA, ACL, or CaseWare for fraud detection.

3. **Data Visualisation Tools:**

    ➢ Tools like Tableau or Power BI create charts and graphs to interpret findings.

4. **AI and Machine Learning Algorithms:**

    ➢ Using predictive models to flag high-risk transactions.

3. Challenges in Data Collection and Analysis

a. Data Volume:

- Large volumes of unstructured data can be overwhelming to process manually.

b. Data Integrity:

- Incomplete or inaccurate records may hinder the investigation.

c. Resistance to Disclosure:

- Employees or external entities may resist sharing critical data.

d. Evolving Technology:

- Rapid changes in digital platforms and fraud techniques require constant adaptation.

4. Real-World Example

Case Study: Fraud in a Retail Chain

Scenario:

A retail chain experienced significant financial losses due to unidentified discrepancies in inventory and sales data.

Actions:

1. Reviewed point-of-sale (POS) system data to identify anomalies.
2. Analysed employee transaction logs and found repeated voided sales linked to a specific employee.
3. Corroborated findings with surveillance footage to confirm fraudulent activity.

Outcome:

The employee was terminated, and the company implemented stricter POS controls and monitoring software.

5. Best Practices in Data Collection and Analysis

- **Adopt Automated Tools:** Use software to streamline data collection and analysis.
- **Ensure Data Confidentiality:** Protect sensitive information during investigations.

- **Regular Training:** Stay updated on fraud techniques and analytical tools.
- **Collaborate Across Departments:** Work with IT, HR, and legal teams for a holistic approach.

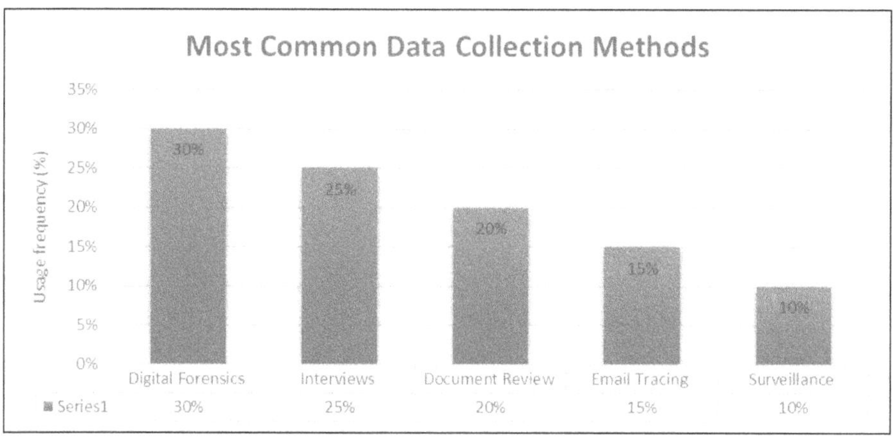

Interviewing Techniques and Red Flags

Interviewing is a core of forensic investigations, providing direct insights into financial activities, motivations, and relationships. Effective interviewing uncovers additional information, corroborates data findings, and can reveal behavioural red flags that indicate deception.

Interviewing is a critical investigative tool in forensic accounting. Proper techniques enable forensic accountants to gather insights, validate evidence, and uncover discrepancies. Understanding red flags—the warning signs of potential fraud—is equally crucial for interpreting the information collected during interviews.

1. **Importance of Interviewing in Forensic Accounting**

Interviews help:

- **Verify Facts:** Cross-check data from financial records.
- **Understand Processes:** Gain insights into workflows and controls that might have been bypassed.

- **Detect Fraudulent Behaviour:** Spot inconsistencies or evasive answers that indicate misconduct.
- **Build a Narrative:** Construct a coherent timeline of events leading to suspected fraud.

2. Interviewing Techniques

a. Preparation

1. **Define Objectives:** Determine what information you need from the interview.

   - Example: Understanding why specific transactions were authorised.

2. **Review Records:** Study relevant documents and data related to the interviewee.
3. **Select the Right Setting:** Choose a private, neutral, and non-intimidating location.

b. Conducting the Interview

1. **Build Rapport:** Start with small talk to put the interviewee at ease.
2. **Ask Open-Ended Questions:** Encourage the interviewee to explain their answers in detail.

   - Example: "Can you walk me through the process of approving vendor payments?"

3. **Probe for Details:** Use follow-up questions to clarify vague responses.

   - Example: "Why was this vendor selected without competitive bidding?"

4. **Maintain Neutrality:** Avoid accusations or leading questions that could bias the answers.

5. **Observe Non-Verbal Cues:** Pay attention to body language, tone, and hesitation, which may indicate deceit.
6. **Use the Funnel Technique:** Start with general questions and narrow down to specifics as the interview progresses.

c. Types of Questions

1. **Introductory Questions:** Set the stage and establish trust.

   - "How long have you been with the company?"

2. **Informational Questions:** Gather relevant details.

   - "What is your role in processing invoices?"

3. **Closing Questions:** Confirm understanding and ensure completeness.

   - "Is there anything else you think I should know?"

3. Documenting the Interview

1. **Take Detailed Notes:** Record key points during the interview.
2. **Audio/Video Recording:** With consent, record the interview for accuracy.
3. **Summarise Findings:** Compile a report highlighting key insights and contradictions.

4. Identifying Red Flags in Interviews

a. Behavioural Red Flags

- **Evasiveness:** Avoiding direct answers or changing the topic.
- **Over justification:** Providing excessive detail for simple questions.
- **Body Language:** Fidgeting, avoiding eye contact, or crossing arms.
- **Inconsistent Statements:** Contradicting previous answers or known facts.

b. Financial Red Flags

- **Unexplained Wealth:** Sudden display of wealth unrelated to known income.
- **High Employee Turnover:** Frequent resignations in specific departments.
- **Unusual Transactions:** Excessive cash transactions or payments to unknown vendors.

c. Operational Red Flags

- **Lack of Documentation:** Missing invoices or incomplete records.
- **Unclear Processes:** Ambiguity in how financial activities are handled.

5. Real-World Example: Uncovering Fraud Through Interviewing

Case Study:
A manufacturing company suspected inventory theft.

Actions:
1. Interviewed employees involved in inventory management.
2. Noticed one employee frequently hesitated when asked about discrepancies in stock levels.
3. Further probing revealed they had been falsifying records to cover up theft.

Outcome:
The employee was terminated, and the company implemented stricter controls, including automated inventory tracking.

6. Best Practices for Effective Interviewing

- **Remain Professional:** Maintain composure and objectivity throughout the interview.
- **Use Empathy:** Show understanding to build trust, but remain focused on the facts.

- **Be Patient:** Allow interviewees time to respond without rushing them.
- **Cross-Verify:** Compare statements with other evidence to confirm accuracy.

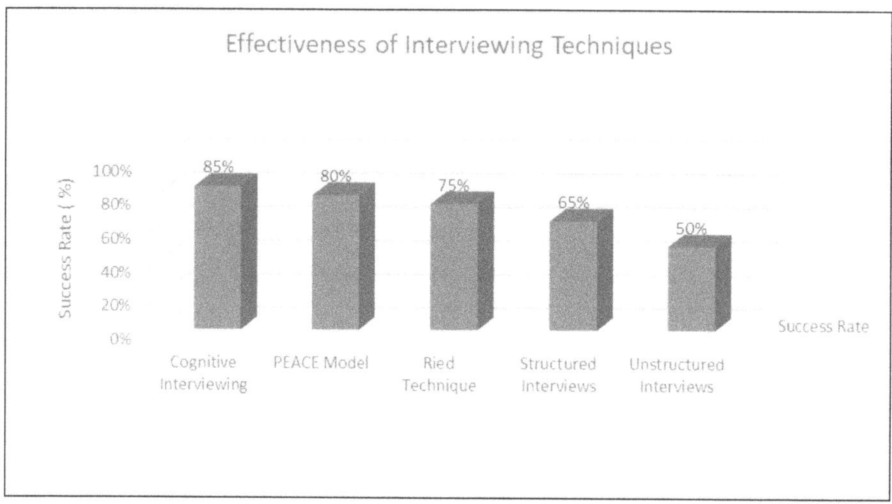

The **"Effectiveness of Interviewing Techniques"** chart compares the success rates of different forensic interviewing methods based on percentage effectiveness.

Key Insights:

- Cognitive Interviewing is the most effective, likely due to its emphasis on memory recall and rapport-building.
- The PEACE Model, widely used in the UK, follows closely with a strong focus on ethical, non-coercive methods.
- Reid Technique remains popular but shows slightly reduced effectiveness, potentially due to criticisms over coercion risks.
- Structured Interviews offer moderate consistency.
- Unstructured Interviews are the least reliable, possibly due to lack of preparation and variability in approach.

Conclusion:

Applying Interview Findings to the Investigation: Insights gathered from interviews can confirm, refute, or expand upon the information collected during the data analysis phase. The findings from these interviews should be cross-referenced with financial records and other evidence, allowing forensic accountants to build a comprehensive and accurate picture of potential misconduct.

Data collection, analysis, and effective interviewing techniques are fundamental to forensic accounting investigations. These skills enable forensic accountants to uncover hidden patterns, gather firsthand insights, and identify behavioural red flags that may indicate fraud or financial misconduct. Mastery of these techniques is essential for constructing credible and thorough reports and for supporting findings in legal proceedings.

Chapter 05

Financial Fraud Detection

"Spotting the Red Flags Before They're Headlines"

Financial fraud represents a critical threat to organisations of all sizes, adversely impacting profitability, reputation, and legal standing. By comprehensively understanding the prevalent types of financial fraud, organisations can more effectively identify their vulnerabilities and implement appropriate preventive measures.

This chapter analyses the common forms of financial fraud. It delineates the red flags or early warning signals that may assist forensic accountants and organisational stakeholders recognise fraudulent activities before they escalate.

1. Common Types of Financial Fraud

Financial fraud includes various deceitful practices aimed at personal or organisational gain. Below are the most common forms:

A. Asset Misappropriation

- **Definition:** Theft or misuse of a company's resources.
- **Examples:**

  - ➢ Skimming: Stealing cash before it is recorded in the books.
  - ➢ Fraudulent expense claims: Inflating or falsifying expenses.
  - ➢ Payroll fraud: Creating ghost employees, inflating overtime hours or manipulating wages.

- **Impact:** Loss of cash or valuable assets, reputational damage.

B. Financial Statement Fraud

- **Definition:** Intentional misrepresentation of financial information.
- **Examples:**

  - ➢ Revenue recognition fraud: Recording revenue prematurely or for non-existent sales.
  - ➢ Understating expenses: Hiding liabilities or inflating profits.
  - ➢ Manipulating reserves: Changing estimates for future expenses to smooth earnings.

- **Impact:** Misleading investors, regulatory penalties, loss of credibility.

C. Corruption

- **Definition:** Abuse of power for personal gain.
- **Examples:**

  - ➢ Bribery: Offering or accepting money or gifts to influence decisions.
  - ➢ Kickbacks: Receiving payment to facilitate deals or transactions.
  - ➢ Conflict of interest: Making decisions to benefit oneself or close associates.

- **Impact:** Damaged trust, legal liabilities, and operational inefficiencies.

D. Cyber Fraud

- **Definition:** Fraud committed using technology or digital platforms.
- **Examples:**

  - ➢ Phishing: Trick employees into revealing sensitive data.
  - ➢ Ransomware: Locks systems and demands payment for access.

> ➢ Payment diversion: Redirecting payments to unauthorised accounts.

- **Impact:** Loss of funds, data breaches, and legal implications.

E. Identity Theft and Impersonation

- Definition: Fraudulent use of personal or business identities.
- Examples:

> ➢ Opening bank accounts or taking out loans in another entity's name.
> ➢ Falsifying tax filings to obtain refunds.

- Impact: Financial loss, damage to creditworthiness, and legal complications.

2. Key Types of Financial Frauds

a. Identity Theft

> ➢ **Definition**: Identity theft involves illegally acquiring and using someone else's personal information, such as Social Security numbers or bank account details, to commit fraud.
> ➢ **Examples**: Phishing attacks, data breaches, and physical theft of personal documents.
> ➢ **Impact**: Victims may face financial losses, damaged credit scores, and legal complications.

b. Payment Fraud

> ➢ **Definition**: Payment fraud occurs when unauthorised transactions use stolen payment information, such as credit card numbers or bank account details.
> ➢ **Examples**: Credit card fraud, unauthorised electronic fund transfers, and counterfeit checks.
> ➢ **Impact**: Financial institutions and consumers may suffer significant financial losses and reputational damage.

c. **Account Takeover Fraud**

- ➢ **Definition**: Account takeover fraud involves gaining unauthorised access to a victim's financial accounts and using them for fraudulent activities.
- ➢ **Examples**: Hacking into online banking accounts, intercepting mail to obtain account information, and using stolen credentials to access accounts.
- ➢ **Impact**: Victims may lose funds, and financial institutions may face increased security costs and customer dissatisfaction.

d. **Advance Fee Fraud**

- ➢ **Definition**: Advance fee fraud involves promising a large sum of money or valuable goods in exchange for an upfront payment, which is never delivered.
- ➢ **Examples**: Lottery scams, inheritance scams, and fake investment opportunities.
- ➢ **Impact**: Victims may lose significant amounts of money and suffer emotional distress.

e. **Credit Card Fraud**

- ➢ **Definition**: Credit card fraud involves unauthorised use of a credit card to purchase or withdraw funds.
- ➢ **Examples**: Skimming devices, online shopping fraud, and fraudulent card-not-present transactions.
- ➢ **Impact**: Cardholders and financial institutions may face financial losses and increased security measures.

f. **Investment Fraud**

- ➢ **Definition**: Investment fraud involves deceiving investors with false information to make them invest in non-existent or worthless assets.

> **Examples**: Ponzi schemes, pump-and-dump schemes, and fake investment opportunities.
> **Impact**: Investors may lose their savings, and the overall trust in financial markets may be undermined.

g. **Consumer Fraud**

> **Definition**: Consumer fraud involves deceptive practices that result in financial or personal gain at the expense of consumers.
> **Examples**: False advertising, bait-and-switch schemes, and fraudulent product claims.
> **Impact**: Consumers may lose money, receive substandard products, and lose business trust.

h. **Fraudulent Charities**

> **Definition**: Fraudulent charities involve creating fake charitable organisations to solicit donations never used for the intended purpose.
> **Examples**: Fake disaster relief funds, bogus medical research charities, and fraudulent crowdfunding campaigns.
> **Impact**: Donors lose money, and legitimate charities may suffer from decreased donations.

i. **Return Fraud**

> **Definition**: Return fraud involves exploiting a retailer's return policy to obtain refunds or exchanges for non-existent or stolen goods.
> **Examples**: Returning stolen items, using counterfeit receipts, and wardrobing (returning used items).
> **Impact**: Retailers face financial losses and may implement stricter return policies.

j. **Chargeback Fraud**

> **Definition**: Chargeback fraud occurs when a consumer disputes a legitimate transaction to obtain a refund while keeping the goods or services.
> **Examples**: Friendly fraud (disputing a legitimate purchase), using stolen credit card information, and exploiting chargeback policies.
> **Impact**: Merchants face financial losses, increased chargeback fees, and potential account closures.

k. **Cybercrime**

> **Definition**: Cybercrime involves using technology to commit financial fraud, such as hacking, phishing, and malware attacks.
> **Examples**: Ransomware attacks, online banking fraud, and identity theft through data breaches.
> **Impact**: Victims may lose funds, personal information, and face long-term financial and reputational damage.

These key types of financial fraud highlight the diverse and evolving nature of fraudulent activities. Understanding these frauds is crucial for implementing effective detection and prevention strategies

Detecting Fraud in Practice

a. Tools and Techniques for Detection

- **Trend and Ratio Analysis:** Identifying unusual patterns in financial performance.
- **Forensic Data Analytics:** Using software to analyse large datasets for anomalies.
- **Transaction Monitoring:** Continuous monitoring of transactions to flag high-risk activities.

b. Case Study: Expense Fraud Detection

- **Scenario:** A company noticed its travel expense claims had significantly increased.
- **Actions Taken:**

  - ✓ Reviewed receipts and documentation.
  - ✓ Discovered duplicate claims submitted with altered dates.
  - ✓ Implemented stricter expense claim policies and automated monitoring.

- **Outcome:** Fraudulent activity was halted, saving the company significant losses.

Preventive Measures for Businesses

- **Regular Audits:** Conduct periodic internal and external audits.
- **Fraud Awareness Training:** Educate employees on red flags and reporting mechanisms.
- **Strengthening Internal Controls:** Ensure segregation of duties and restricted access.
- **Adopting Technology:** Use fraud detection tools to monitor and analyse data.

Real-World Example: Financial Statement Fraud

Case: A multinational company overstated its revenue by $5 billion over three years.

Key Findings:

1. Fraudulent contracts with fake customers.
2. Underreported liabilities to inflate earnings.

Resolution:
Whistleblower reports revealed the fraud, which resulted in criminal charges and a total overhaul of the company's financial controls.

Key Takeaways

- Financial fraud is diverse and evolving, requiring constant vigilance.
- Red flags provide valuable clues but require thorough investigation.
- Combining technology, strong controls, and skilled personnel is essential for fraud detection and prevention.

Red Flags and Early Warning Signs

Recognising the early warning signs of financial fraud can help prevent significant losses. Red flags are indicators that something may be amiss, prompting a deeper investigation. While these signs do not always confirm fraud, they highlight areas requiring attention.

Detecting fraud early necessitates a keen understanding of the warning signs. These can be categorised as follows:

Common Red Flags of Financial Fraud:

A. Unusual Transactions and Patterns:

- **Unexplained Increases in Expenses:** Unexpected spikes in costs, especially in areas like travel, supplies, or entertainment, could signal misappropriation.
- **High Volume of Adjusting Entries:** Frequent adjustments to financial records may indicate attempts to manipulate accounts.
- **Unusual Vendor Payments:** Payments to unknown or unverified vendors, or payments that do not align with business needs, can suggest fraud.

B. Employee Behaviour and Lifestyle Changes:

- **Lifestyle Discrepancies:** Sudden or unexplained improvements in lifestyle, such as expensive purchases, vacations, or luxury items, may indicate misappropriated funds.

> ➢ **Resistance to Supervision**: Employees who refuse oversight or are secretive about their work could hide fraudulent activities.

> ➢ **Behavioural Red Flags**: Excessive defensiveness, reluctance to take vacations, or unwillingness to share responsibilities could signal potential fraud.

C. Accounting Irregularities:

> ➢ **Unbalanced or Inconsistent Financial Statements**: Discrepancies between reported and actual figures often indicate financial statement fraud.

> ➢ **Frequent Manual Entries or Overrides**: Frequent manual adjustments to records or overrides of controls can be used to manipulate financial data.

> ➢ **Missing Documentation**: Invoices, receipts, or other documentation missing without explanation could indicate an attempt to hide fraudulent transactions.

D. Vendor and Supplier Relationships:

> ➢ **Unverified Vendors**: Transactions with vendors lacking complete information or appearing in unusual locations can indicate fictitious suppliers.

> ➢ **High Dependence on a Single Supplier**: Relying heavily on one supplier, especially if prices seem inflated, can signify kickbacks or corruption.

> ➢ **Unusual Payment Terms**: Payment patterns that deviate from usual business practices, such as early or expedited payments, may signal kickbacks or bribes.

E. Banking and Cash Flow Issues:

> ➢ **Unexplained Cash Flow Shortages**: Frequent cash flow issues without a clear cause may indicate misappropriation of funds.

> ➤ **Irregular Bank Reconciliation**: Discrepancies between bank records and internal accounts should be investigated for potential theft or manipulation.
>
> ➤ **Suspicious Withdrawals or Transfers**: Large or frequent transfers to unknown accounts could indicate misappropriation.

The Role of Forensic Accountants in Identifying Red Flags: Forensic accountants employ their skills to detect red flags early, thereby preventing financial fraud from escalating. They merge analytical techniques, investigative methods, and accounting expertise to identify unusual patterns, interview employees, and track the source of discrepancies.

Establishing Fraud Prevention Protocols Based on Red Flags: Recognising these warning signs assists organisations in strengthening their internal controls. By developing fraud prevention protocols, such as mandatory vacations, regular audits, and separation of duties, businesses can establish a more robust defence against fraud.

Common Red Flags of Financial Fraud are further explained:

1. **Unusual Transactions**

    - **Definition**: Transactions that deviate significantly from normal business operations or personal spending patterns.
    - **Examples**: Large, round-number transactions, frequent small withdrawals, or transfers to unknown accounts.
    - **Impact**: These anomalies can indicate fraudulent activities such as embezzlement or money laundering.

2. **Inconsistent Financial Records**

    - **Definition**: Discrepancies between financial statements, bank records, and supporting documents.
    - **Examples**: Mismatched invoices, unexplained adjustments, or missing documentation.

- **Impact**: Inconsistencies can signal manipulation of financial data to conceal fraud.

3. **Unexplained Changes in Lifestyle**

   - **Definition**: Significant changes in an individual's lifestyle that are not consistent with their known income.
   - **Examples**: Sudden acquisition of luxury items, expensive vacations, or unexplained wealth.
   - **Impact**: Such changes may indicate that the individual is benefiting from fraudulent activities.

4. **Frequent Complaints from Customers or Vendors**

   - **Definition**: An increase in complaints related to billing, payments, or product quality.
   - **Examples**: Discrepancies in invoices, delayed payments, or unauthorised charges.
   - **Impact**: Frequent complaints can highlight underlying fraudulent practices within the organisation.

5. **High Employee Turnover**

   - **Definition**: A rapid or unusual rate of employee departures, especially in key financial positions.
   - **Examples**: Frequent resignations or terminations in the accounting or finance departments.
   - **Impact**: High turnover can indicate a toxic work environment or attempts to cover up fraudulent activities.

6. **Reluctance to Share Financial Information**

   - **Definition**: Hesitation or refusal to provide access to financial records or cooperate with audits.
   - **Examples**: Delayed responses to information requests, restricted access to certain documents, or evasive behaviour.

- **Impact**: Reluctance to share information can be a red flag for attempts to hide fraudulent activities.

7. **Unusual Vendor Relationships**

   - **Definition**: Suspicious or unexplained relationships with vendors or suppliers.
   - **Examples**: Payments to unknown or unverified vendors, frequent changes in suppliers, or unusually favourable terms.
   - **Impact**: Unusual vendor relationships can indicate kickbacks, bribery, or other fraudulent schemes.

8. **Excessive Pressure to Meet Targets**

   - **Definition**: Intense pressure on employees to achieve financial targets or performance goals.
   - **Examples**: Unrealistic sales targets, aggressive revenue projections, or threats of job loss for underperformance.
   - **Impact**: Excessive pressure can lead employees to engage in fraudulent activities to meet expectations.

9. **Complex or Opaque Financial Structures**

   - **Definition**: Use of overly complex or non-transparent financial arrangements.
   - **Examples**: Multiple shell companies, off-balance-sheet transactions, or convoluted ownership structures.
   - **Impact**: Complexity and opacity can be used to obscure fraudulent activities and evade detection.

10. **Unusual Patterns in Financial Ratios**

    - **Definition**: Significant deviations in key financial ratios from industry norms or historical trends.
    - **Examples**: Abnormal profit margins, liquidity ratios, or debt-to-equity ratios.

- **Impact**: Unusual patterns in financial ratios can indicate manipulation of financial statements to hide fraud.

11. **Frequent Adjustments or Write-Offs**

- **Definition**: Regular or unexplained adjustments to financial statements or frequent write-offs.
- **Examples**: Large bad debt write-offs, frequent inventory adjustments, or unexplained expense entries.
- **Impact**: Frequent adjustments can signify attempts to conceal fraudulent activities or financial mismanagement.

These common red flags can help identify potential financial fraud early. By remaining vigilant and recognising these warning signs, businesses can take proactive steps to investigate and prevent fraud.

This **chart** visually breaks down the **most common types of financial fraud** across five major industries: Finance, Healthcare, Retail, Manufacturing, and Government. The outer ring shows specific fraud types and their respective percentages, nested within the inner ring representing the industries. Here's a detailed summary of what the chart conveys:

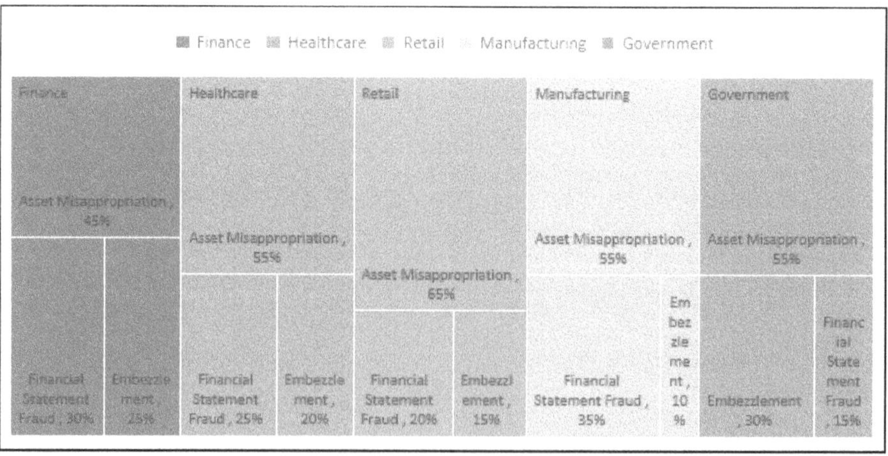

Finance Sector:

- **Asset Misappropriation (45%)**
  This includes theft or misuse of company assets like cash, inventory, or equipment.

- **Financial Statement Fraud (30%)**
  Involves manipulation of financial reports to mislead stakeholders (e.g., inflating revenue).

- **Embezzlement (25%)**
  Refers to internal staff illegally diverting funds for personal use.

Insight: The finance sector sees a balanced mix of all three fraud types, with asset misappropriation being the most common.

Healthcare Sector:

- **Asset Misappropriation (55%)**
  Often includes billing for unprovided services or stealing medical supplies.

- **Embezzlement (20%)**
  Staff or administrators may reroute patient payments or insurance claims.

- **Financial Statement Fraud (not clearly shown but minimal)**

Insight: Asset misappropriation is overwhelmingly the most prevalent fraud type in healthcare, often tied to weak internal controls.

Retail Sector:

- **Asset Misappropriation (65%)**
  Includes inventory theft, fake returns, or skimming cash from registers.

Insight: Retail is highly vulnerable to asset misappropriation due to high transaction volumes and inventory handling.

Manufacturing Sector:

- **Asset Misappropriation (55%)**
  Examples include misusing raw materials or machinery for personal gain.

- **Financial Statement Fraud (35%)**
  Misrepresenting production costs, sales, or inventory figures.

Insight: Both operational fraud (asset misuse) and reporting fraud are key concerns in manufacturing.

Government Sector:

- **Asset Misappropriation (55%)**
  Fraudulent use of government resources—such as vehicles, grants, or materials.

- **Embezzlement (30%)**
  Misuse of public funds by insiders.

- **Financial Statement Fraud (not shown clearly, but likely minimal)**

Insight: Government agencies are also prone to internal fraud due to bureaucracy and oversight gaps.

Overall Insights:

- **Asset misappropriation is the most widespread fraud type across all sectors, with the highest percentage in the retail sector (65%) and government sector (55%).**
- **Fraud in financial Statements is more prominent in finance and manufacturing,** likely due to regulatory pressures and performance reporting.
- **Embezzlement** is notable in **Finance, Healthcare,** and **Government,** pointing to internal control weaknesses.

Conclusion:

Identifying the various types of financial fraud, such as embezzlement, money laundering, and insider trading, along with recognising specific red flags, is crucial for effective fraud detection. Understanding how these fraudulent activities manifest, such as unusual transactions, discrepancies in financial records, or sudden changes in employee behaviour, enables forensic accountants and business professionals to take proactive measures. By remaining vigilant and analytical, they can significantly reduce the potential for fraud, protect valuable assets, and ensure the transparency and integrity of financial operations in their organisations. This thorough approach safeguards against immediate risks and fosters a culture of ethical practice and accountability within the workplace.

Chapter 06

Analytical Tools and Software

"Technology as an Ally in Fraud Detection"

Tools and Technology Used in Forensic Accounting

Introduction to Analytical Tools in Forensic Accounting: As financial fraud becomes increasingly sophisticated, forensic accountants depend on advanced tools and software to analyse vast amounts of data, uncover hidden patterns, and efficiently identify fraudulent activities. These tools enhance the accuracy and speed of investigations, providing insights that manual analysis alone may overlook.

Key Types of Tools and Technology in Forensic Accounting:

Data Analytics and Visualisation Software:

A. <u>**Using Microsoft Excel for Fraud Detection**</u>: Microsoft Excel is commonly used for data manipulation, statistical analysis, and creating visualizations that aid in detecting trends and anomalies. Employing tools like Microsoft Excel can significantly enhance fraud detection and prevention efforts.

   a. **Data Analysis and Visualisation:**

   ➢ **Pivot Tables**: Create pivot tables to summarise large datasets and identify trends or anomalies.

   ➢ **Conditional Formatting**: Use conditional formatting to highlight unusual transactions or outliers.

   ➢ **Formulas and Functions**: Utilise formulas like SUMIFS, COUNTIFS, and FREQUENCY to analyse transaction patterns and detect discrepancies.

b. **Benford's Law:**

> ➤ **Leading Digit Analysis**: Apply Benford's Law to analyse the frequency distribution of leading digits in your data. This can help identify fabricated numbers or manipulated data.
> ➤ **Charts and Graphs**: Create charts to visualise the expected vs. actual distribution of leading digits.

c. **Data Validation:**

> ➤ Data Validation Rules: Establish data validation rules to ensure data integrity and prevent errors.
> ➤ Error Checking: Utilise Excel's error-checking features to identify and correct inconsistencies in your data.

B. **Using Power BI for Fraud Detection:** Power BI is a data visualisation and reporting tool made by Microsoft. Think of it like a smart dashboard builder that helps you turn raw data into easy-to-read charts, graphs, and reports. Understand trends and patterns in your business or data. View reports on your computer, tablet, or phone — anywhere

In Everyday Terms: Imagine you have lots of data in Excel or from a website or software. Power BI helps you: Pull all that data together, clean it up, make colourful dashboards with graphs, maps, and tables, and share it with your team or clients in just a few clicks.

a. **Data Integration:**

> ➤ **Data Import**: Import data from various sources, such as databases, spreadsheets, and APIs, into Power BI.
> ➤ **Data Transformation**: Cleanse and transform data to ensure accuracy and consistency.

b. **Interactive Dashboards:**

➤ **Visualisations:** Create interactive dashboards with visualisations like scatter plots, heat maps, and bar charts to identify patterns and anomalies.

➤ **Real-Time Monitoring:** Set up real-time monitoring to track transactions and flag suspicious activities immediately.

c. **Advanced Analytics:**

➤ **Predictive Analytics:** Use predictive analytics to identify potential fraud patterns based on historical data.

➤ **Machine Learning Models:** Implement machine learning models to enhance fraud detection capabilities.

d. **Reporting and Compliance:**

➤ **Audit Trails:** Generate audit trails and compliance reports to ensure adherence to regulatory standards.

➤ **Custom Alerts:** Set up custom alerts to notify stakeholders of potential fraud incidents.

By combining Excel's and Power BI's capabilities, you can create a robust fraud detection and prevention system that helps safeguard your organization's financial integrity.

C. <u>Tableau:</u> was developed in 2003 by **Christian Chabot, Pat Hanrahan and Chris Stolte** At **Stanford University** (as part of a computer science project). In 2019, Salesforce, a major cloud software company, acquired Tableau.

It is a data visualisation tool that enables forensic accountants to create dynamic reports, dashboards, and visuals that illustrate complex data patterns and outliers. Tableau is a powerful fraud detection and prevention tool due to its robust data visualisation and analytics capabilities. Here's how you can use Tableau to enhance your fraud detection efforts:

Using Tableau for Fraud Detection and Prevention

a. **Data Integration:**

> ➤ **Connect to Data Sources:** Import data from various sources such as databases, spreadsheets, and APIs into Tableau.
> ➤ **Data Cleansing:** Cleanse and transform data to ensure accuracy and consistency.

b. **Interactive Dashboards:**

> ➤ **Visualisations:** Create interactive dashboards featuring visualisations such as scatter plots, heat maps, and bar charts to identify patterns and anomalies.
> ➤ **Real-Time Monitoring:** Establish real-time monitoring to track transactions and promptly flag suspicious activities.

c. **Advanced Analytics:**

> ➤ **Predictive Analytics:** Employ predictive analytics to uncover potential fraud patterns derived from historical data.
> ➤ **Machine Learning Models:** Implement machine learning models to enhance fraud detection capabilities.

d. **Identifying Fraud Risk Factors:**

> ➤ **Risk Assessment:** Take a moment to document and review your organization's anti-fraud risk program. It's an important step to ensure everything is in order!
> ➤ **Fraud Risk Factors:** Let's take a moment to identify and prioritise areas vulnerable to fraud schemes.

e. **Analysing Data:**

- ➢ **Mix, Match, and Analyse**: Mix, match, and analyse data from different sources to uncover hidden patterns and red flags.
- ➢ **Benford's Law**: Apply Benford's Law to detect anomalies in numerical data.

f. **Sharing Insights and Alerts:**

- ➢ **Insights Sharing**: Share insights with stakeholders and schedule alerts for potential fraud incidents.
- ➢ **Actionable Insights**: Provide actionable insights to help stakeholders take preventive measures.

g. **Proactive Risk Management:**

- ➢ **Proactive Approach**: Take a proactive approach to exposing risk and ensuring compliance by exploring all financial data.
- ➢ **Flagging Suspicious Activity**: Use Tableau to flag suspicious activities and alert stakeholders before it's too late.

By leveraging Tableau's powerful analytics and visualisation capabilities, you can create a robust fraud detection and prevention system that helps safeguard your organisation's financial integrity.

D. <u>SAS</u>: **SAS** stands for Statistical Analysis System. Today, it's developed and maintained by **SAS Institute Inc.**, co-founded by **James Goodnight**, who also served as its long-time CEO. SAS is a powerful software suite for analysing large amounts of data. It is Advanced statistical software often used in forensic investigations for more sophisticated data analysis and predictive modelling.

Using SAS for Fraud Detection and Prevention

SAS offers a comprehensive fraud detection and prevention tool suite, leveraging advanced analytics, machine learning, and real-time monitoring. Here's how you can use SAS to enhance your fraud detection efforts:

a. **Data Integration**:

➤ **Combine Data Sources**: Integrate internal, external, and third-party data to create a comprehensive dataset for analysis.

➤ **Data Cleansing**: Cleanse and transform data to ensure accuracy and consistency.

b. **Real-Time Monitoring**:

➤ **Transaction Scoring**: Score 100% of transactions in real-time using in-memory processing, delivering high throughput and low-latency response times.

➤ **Anomaly Detection**: Employ embedded machine learning methods to detect and adapt to changing behaviour patterns, identifying anomalies and potential fraud.

c. **Predictive Analytics**:

➤ **Predictive Models**: Develop predictive models to identify potential fraud patterns using historical data.

➤ **Risk Profiling**: Develop risk profiles for transactions and entities to evaluate the likelihood of fraudulent activities.

d. **Fraud Management**:

➤ **End-to-end Solution**: Implement an end-to-end fraud management solution that supports multiple channels and lines of business.

➢ **Signature-Based Approach**: Use a patented signature-based approach to capture customer behaviour data and analyse it for patterns and inconsistencies.

e. **Customer Experience**:

➢ **Reduce False Positives**: Improve fraud detection capabilities and reduce false positives, leading to fewer customer inconveniences.

➢ **Immediate Alerts**: Generate scored and prioritised alerts, enabling immediate customer self-service or fast review and assessment.

E. <u>**Using R for Fraud Detection and Prevention:**</u>

Ross Ihaka and Robert Gentleman created R at the **University of Auckland** in **New Zealand** in the early 1990s. R is a powerful programming language for statistical computing and graphics, widely used for data analysis and visualisation. Here's how you can use R for fraud detection and prevention:

a. **Data Analysis**:

➢ **Statistical Techniques**: Use statistical techniques such as logistic regression, decision trees, and artificial neural networks (ANN) to develop effective fraud detection models.

➢ **Pattern Recognition**: Identify patterns and anomalies in transaction data using machine learning algorithms.

b. **Predictive Analytics**:

➢ **Predictive Models**: Build predictive models to forecast potential fraud based on historical data.

➢ **Machine Learning**: Implement machine learning techniques to enhance fraud detection accuracy and efficiency.

c. **Real-Time Monitoring**:

> - **Real-Time Analysis**: Perform real-time analysis of transactions and user behaviour to detect fraud as it happens.
> - **Proactive Prevention**: Use real-time monitoring to take proactive measures against potential fraud.

d. **Visualisation**:

> - **Data Visualisation**: Create visualisations such as scatter plots, heat maps, and bar charts to identify trends and anomalies in the data.
> - **Interactive Dashboards**: Develop interactive dashboards to present findings and monitor fraud indicators in real time.

By leveraging SAS and R's capabilities, you can create a robust fraud detection and prevention system that helps safeguard your organisation's financial integrity.

I. Forensic Accounting Software:

These specialised forensic accounting tools examine and analyse large datasets, helping forensic accountants identify irregularities, duplications, and suspicious patterns within transactional data.

A. **IDEA (Interactive Data Extraction and Analysis)**

Developed by CaseWare International Inc., a Canadian software company. **IDEA** is a powerful forensic accounting software designed by audit experts to help detect fraud, identify anomalies, and analyse financial data. Here are some key features:

- **Data Import**: Seamlessly imports data from various sources, including PDFs, Excel files, CSVs, and over 50 accounting packages like QuickBooks and Sage.

- **Audit Analytics**: Provides comprehensive audit analytics tools for tasks such as sampling, automated tests, and detailed analysis.
- **Interactive Dashboards**: Visually pinpoint patterns, trends, and outliers using interactive dashboards.
- **Project Overview**: This tool displays the status of every task using sleek graphics, ensuring a transparent project management process.
- **Reporting**: Generates detailed reports that document findings and support conclusions.

B. **ACL Analytics (Audit Command Language)**

Initially developed by ACL Services Ltd., founded by Harold Macintosh and based in Vancouver, Canada, in 1987.

ACL Analytics is another robust forensic accounting tool used primarily for data analysis in auditing and forensic investigations. Key features include:

- **Data Analysis**: Allows users to manipulate large datasets efficiently to identify patterns, anomalies, and potential fraud.
- **Automated Data Entry**: This method automates data entry using optical character recognition (OCR) and intelligent document processing, enhancing accuracy and reliability.
- **Advanced Data Analysis**: This site provides tools for advanced data analysis, including interactive charts, heat maps, and network diagrams.
- **Case Management**: Manages complex cases from initial assignment to final resolution, facilitating seamless teamwork.
- **Compliance Support**: Ensures adherence to various laws and regulations, including financial crime investigations related to the Bank Secrecy Act (BSA).

Both IDEA and ACL Analytics are essential tools for forensic accountants. They help them uncover financial irregularities and provide solid evidence in legal proceedings.

C. **QuickBooks, Xero and Zoho**: Popular accounting platforms that include auditing and report generation features, often used in smaller investigations or to verify general accounting practices.

1. **QuickBooks for Forensic Accounting**

   QuickBooks is a widely used accounting software that can be a valuable tool for forensic accountants. Here are some ways it can be used for fraud detection and prevention:

   a. **Audit Trail**: QuickBooks has a built-in audit trail feature that logs every transaction, including additions, deletions, and modifications. This can help forensic accountants track changes and identify suspicious activities

   b. **Transaction Analysis**: Forensic accountants can detect anomalies and potential fraud by analysing transaction patterns and comparing them against expected behaviours.

   c. **User Access**: QuickBooks allows for different levels of user access, which can help in identifying unauthorised access or changes made by specific users.

   d. **Report Generation**: QuickBooks can generate detailed reports documenting financial activities, making reviewing and analysing data for signs of fraud easier.

2. **Xero for Forensic Accounting**

   Xero is another popular accounting software that offers features beneficial for forensic accounting:

   a. **Real-Time Data**: Xero provides real-time financial data, which allows forensic accountants to monitor transactions and detect fraud as it happens.

   b. **Integration with Other Tools**: Xero can integrate with various tools and apps, such as DocuClipper, which can automate data extraction and enhance analysis.

c. **Detailed Reports**: Xero generates comprehensive financial reports that can be used to identify discrepancies and potential fraudulent activities.

d. **User Permissions**: Similar to QuickBooks, Xero allows for setting user permissions, helping forensic accountants track who made specific changes or transactions.

3. **Zoho Books** is a versatile accounting software that can be highly beneficial for forensic accounting. Here are some key features that make it useful for fraud detection and prevention:

a. **Audit Trail**: Zoho Books maintains a detailed audit trail that logs every transaction, including additions, deletions, and modifications. This helps forensic accountants track changes and identify suspicious activities.

b. **Expense Tracking**: The software allows for digital capture of expense receipts, categorisation, and tracking expenses, which helps identify irregular spending patterns.

c. **User Permissions**: Zoho Books allows for setting different levels of user permissions, making it easier to monitor who made specific changes or transactions.

d. **Real-Time Data**: Provides real-time financial data, enabling forensic accountants to monitor transactions and detect fraud as it happens.

e. **Integration with Other Tools**: Zoho Books can integrate with various tools and apps, enhancing data analysis capabilities.

f. **Detailed Reports**: Generates comprehensive financial reports that can be used to identify discrepancies and potential fraudulent activities.

g. **Document Management**: Allows for organising and accessing essential documents, attaching receipts to expenses or bills, and enabling auto-scan for quick transaction creation.

By leveraging these features, forensic accountants can detect and prevent fraud, ensuring an organisation's financial integrity. All three above—QuickBooks, Zoho, and Xero—offer robust features that can aid forensic accountants in detecting and preventing fraud.

II. Digital Forensics Tools:

A. EnCase: Widely Used for Collecting and Preserving Digital Evidence

EnCase is a comprehensive digital forensics tool developed by Guidance Software (now part of OpenText). Law enforcement, government agencies, and corporate investigators widely use it to collect and preserve digital evidence. Here are some key features:

- **Data Acquisition**: EnCase can acquire data from various devices, including Windows, Mac, Linux, and over 35,000 mobile device profiles.
- **Deep Forensic Analysis**: It performs disk-level analysis and parses data to uncover hidden evidence.
- **Audit Trail**: Maintains a detailed audit trail to ensure the integrity of the evidence collected.
- **Cloud Support**: Can collect evidence from cloud-based applications like social media, storage, and communication tools.
- **Reporting**: Generates detailed reports that are accepted in court.

B. FTK (Forensic Toolkit): Comprehensive Digital Forensics Tool

FTK (Forensic Toolkit), developed by AccessData, is another powerful digital forensics tool for analysing emails, documents, images, and other digital files. Key features include:

- **Data Processing**: Processes and indexes data upfront, allowing faster searches and analysis.

- **Artifact Recovery**: Recovers deleted data and analyses digital evidence from various sources.
- **Mobile Device Support**: Supports native unprocessed extractions from mobile devices.
- **Collaborative Analysis**: Facilitates collaborative case analysis with web-based case management.
- **Custom Scripts**: Allows for the creation of custom Python scripts to automate tasks.

C. **Magnet AXIOM: Examining Data from Various Digital Devices**

Magnet AXIOM is a digital investigation platform that helps forensic examiners recover, analyse, and report on digital evidence from multiple sources. Key features include:

- **Multi-Device Support**: Examines data from mobile devices, computers, cloud storage, and vehicles.
- **Artifact Recovery**: Recovers deleted data and analyses digital evidence with an artifact-first approach.
- **Integrated Analysis**: Processes and analyses data from various sources in one case file.
- **Automated Workflows**: Automates acquisition and processing tasks to save time.
- **Reporting**: Provides customisable report views to share findings easily.

These tools are essential for forensic investigators to uncover digital evidence and provide solid proof in legal proceedings.

Fraud Detection and Transaction Monitoring Systems

CaseWare IDEA

CaseWare IDEA is a comprehensive data analysis software for audit, accounting, and fraud detection. It allows forensic accountants to import data from various sources, including PDFs, Excel files, and CSVs. IDEA offers powerful audit analytics, including tests for Benford's Law, fuzzy duplicate detection, and gap detection. It also provides interactive dashboards for visualising patterns, trends, and outliers3. The software enhances productivity by automating data analysis and improving risk management through machine learning techniques.

SAS Anti-Money Laundering (AML)

SAS Anti-Money Laundering (AML) is a solution designed to detect and prevent money laundering activities. It uses advanced analytics and machine learning to monitor transactions and identify complex threats like virtual currencies and human trafficking. SAS AML offers integrated customer due diligence and enhanced due diligence capabilities, ensuring compliance with regulatory requirements. The system also provides a user-friendly interface for managing investigations and reporting.

FICO Falcon

FICO Falcon Fraud Manager is a real-time transaction monitoring system that detects and prevents fraud across various channels, including credit cards, debit cards, and digital payments. Falcon leverages AI and machine learning to analyse transaction data and identify fraudulent activities. The system includes patented analytic technology and a robust rules engine for defining and deploying anti-fraud rules. Falcon's predictive insights help reduce false positives and enhance customer experience.

Machine Learning and Artificial Intelligence (AI) Tools

IBM Watson

IBM Watson is an AI-driven tool that assists forensic accountants in identifying patterns and predicting potential fraudulent behaviour. Watson uses machine learning algorithms to analyse large datasets and uncover hidden patterns and anomalies. It helps organisations improve their fraud detection capabilities by providing actionable insights and predictive analytics.

Google Cloud AutoML and TensorFlow

Google Cloud AutoML and **TensorFlow** enable forensic accountants to build custom AI models for fraud detection. These tools allow users to detect complex fraud patterns, such as unusual transaction sequences and outlier behaviours. AutoML provides a user-friendly interface for building and deploying machine learning models, while TensorFlow offers powerful libraries for developing and training AI models.

These systems and tools enhance fraud detection and transaction monitoring capabilities, helping organisations prevent fraudulent activities and maintain regulatory compliance.

Emerging Technologies in Forensic Accounting

Blockchain Analysis Tools

How Blockchain Helps Forensic Auditors

Blockchain technology can be a powerful tool for forensic auditors by providing a transparent, immutable record of all transactions. Here's how it can aid in fraud detection and forensic investigations:

1. **Transparency and Traceability:**

   Blockchain's transparency allows forensic auditors to trace all transactions in real time. Every transaction is recorded and publicly available, making it easier to identify suspicious activities and follow the money trail.

2. **Immutable Records:**

   The immutability of blockchain ensures that once data is recorded, it cannot be tampered with. This feature is crucial for forensic auditors as it guarantees the integrity of the financial records, providing reliable evidence for investigations.

3. **Automated Audit Trails:**

Blockchain automatically creates an audit trail for every transaction, including who initiated it, when it was executed, and how much was involved. This audit trail simplifies the process of tracking and verifying transactions.

4. **Smart Contracts:**

Smart contracts are self-executing contracts with the terms directly written into code. They automatically execute and enforce agreements based on predefined conditions. Forensic auditors can use smart contracts to monitor compliance and detect real-time breaches.

5. **Reduced Fraud Risk:**

Blockchain reduces the risk of fraud by providing a secure and transparent record-keeping system. Any attempt to alter a transaction would require altering all subsequent blocks, making fraud detection easier and more reliable.

6. **Enhanced Data Security:**

Blockchain's cryptographic security ensures that sensitive financial information is protected. This reduces the risk of data breaches and unauthorised access, providing a more secure environment for financial transactions.

Practical Applications in Forensic Auditing

1. **Transaction Monitoring:**

Forensic auditors can monitor blockchain transactions for unusual patterns or deviations from normal behaviour that could indicate fraud.

2. **Evidence Collection:**

   The immutable nature of blockchain makes it an excellent source of evidence in legal proceedings. Forensic auditors can collect and present blockchain data as reliable proof of financial activities.

3. **Compliance Verification:**

   Blockchain can verify compliance with financial regulations by providing a transparent record of all transactions. This enables auditors to ensure that businesses adhere to legal requirements.

4. **Asset Tracing:**

   Forensic auditors can trace the movement of assets across the blockchain, aiding in the recovery of misappropriated funds and identifying parties involved in fraudulent activities.

By leveraging blockchain technology, forensic auditors can improve their capacity to detect, investigate, and prevent financial fraud. Blockchain's transparent, immutable, and secure nature makes it an invaluable tool in forensic accounting.

Robotic Process Automation (RPA)

Robotic Process Automation (RPA) software like UiPath and Blue Prism automates repetitive and time-consuming tasks, allowing forensic accountants to focus on higher-level analysis. Here's how RPA can be used:

- **Data Entry**: RPA bots can automate data entry tasks, reducing the risk of human error and increasing efficiency.
- **Reconciliation**: Bots can perform reconciliation tasks, comparing data from different sources to identify discrepancies.
- **Report Generation**: RPA can generate standardised reports, saving time and ensuring consistency.

- **Compliance Monitoring**: Automated workflows can monitor compliance with regulatory requirements, flagging any deviations for further investigation.

By leveraging these emerging technologies, forensic accountants can enhance their capabilities in detecting and preventing financial fraud, ensuring more efficient and accurate investigations.

Case Studies on the Use of Analytical Tools

Case Study 1:

Using Data Analytics to Detect Revenue Recognition Fraud

Background: A mid-sized manufacturing company was suspected of inflating revenue to meet shareholder expectations. Forensic accountants were hired to verify the financial statements and detect potential fraud.

Tools Used:

- **IDEA and Microsoft Power BI**: IDEA was used to extract and analyse transaction-level data from the company's accounting system. Power BI visualisations helped identify revenue spikes that deviated from typical sales patterns.

Findings:

- The analysis revealed unusually high revenue entries at the end of each fiscal quarter, followed by immediate returns or cancellations at the beginning of the following quarter—clear signs of revenue recognition fraud.

Outcome:

- With this evidence, the company's executives could pursue legal action, and adjustments were made to ensure compliance with proper accounting standards in future financial reports.

Case Study 2:

Digital Forensics in Cyber Fraud Investigation

Background: An employee at a tech company was suspected of embezzling funds and deleting evidence from their work computer. A forensic accountant was brought in to investigate.

Tools Used:

- **FTK and EnCase**: FTK was used to recover deleted files, and EnCase preserved the integrity of digital evidence by creating a secure copy of the hard drive.

Findings:

- The forensic team uncovered emails and transaction records showing unauthorised transfers to an offshore account. Deleted invoices and expense records were also recovered, linking the employee directly to the fraud.

Outcome:

- The digital evidence provided enough proof for prosecution, and the company strengthened its internal controls to prevent similar fraud in the future.

Case Study 3:

Detecting Money Laundering with Machine Learning Tools

Background: A financial institution noticed suspicious patterns in client transactions and suspected money laundering activities. Forensic accountants specialising in AML were consulted.

Tools Used:

- **SAS Anti-Money Laundering and IBM Watson**: SAS AML monitored and flagged suspicious transactions, while IBM Watson analysed patterns to detect connections between accounts involved in money laundering schemes.

Findings:

- Machine learning algorithms identified a network of accounts involved in complex layering schemes, where funds were transferred among multiple accounts to obscure their origin. Watson's AI capabilities provided insights into transactional behaviours that traditional methods might have missed.

Outcome:

- The financial institution filed a report with regulatory authorities, leading to an official investigation. The case highlighted the effectiveness of AI in detecting sophisticated financial crime.

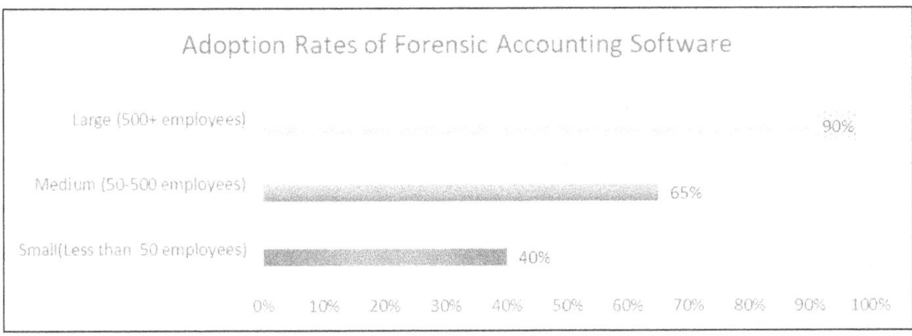

This **horizontal bar chart** presents forensic accounting software adoption rates among businesses of different sizes, categorised by employee count. It highlights how larger businesses are more likely to implement forensic accounting tools than smaller ones.

Large Enterprises (500+ employees):

- **Adoption Rate: 90%**
- **Interpretation:**

Nearly all large organisations have adopted forensic accounting software, showing high awareness of fraud risks and strong investment in compliance, internal controls, and technology. Their complex operations and exposure to fraud risks make such tools essential.

Medium-Sized Enterprises (50–500 employees):

- **Adoption Rate: 65%**
- **Interpretation:**

A majority of mid-sized firms use forensic accounting tools, though adoption lags behind large enterprises. These companies may be growing and more conscious of fraud, but may face budget or integration challenges that hinder full adoption.

Small Enterprises (Less than 50 employees):

- **Adoption Rate: 40%**
- **Interpretation:**

Adoption is relatively low among small businesses, likely due to limited budgets, lack of awareness, or the perception that their fraud risk is low. However, these businesses may still face significant losses if fraud occurs and could benefit from lightweight forensic tools.

Key Insights:

- There is a **clear correlation between company size and software adoption**: the larger the enterprise, the higher the likelihood of using forensic tools.
- **Resource availability** (funds, IT support, training) and **risk perception** appear to be major drivers of adoption.
- The **gap between small (40%) and large businesses (90%)** reveals opportunities for education and scaled-down software solutions tailored for SMEs.

The following bar chart compares the effectiveness of various forensic tools in detecting fraud based on percentage success rates. The tools range from cutting-edge technologies like AI to traditional auditing software. The graph provides a clear performance ranking of these tools.

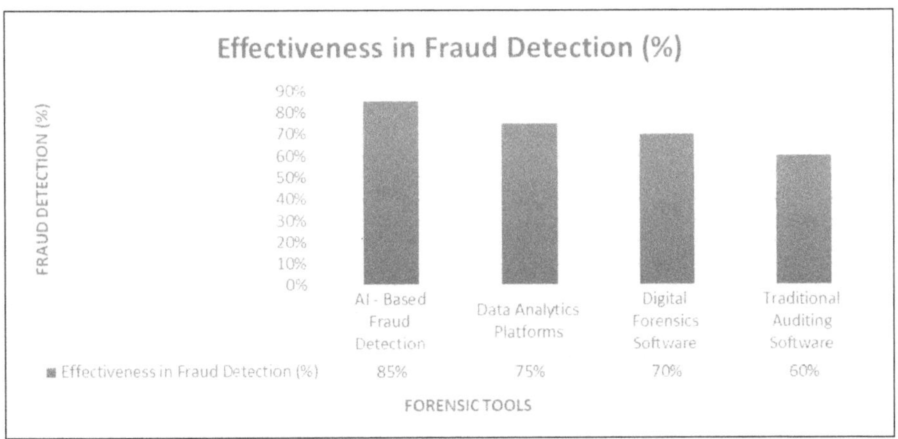

Tool-wise Breakdown:

1. AI-Based Fraud Detection

- **Effectiveness: 85%**
- **Interpretation:**

  This is the **most effective tool**, significantly outperforming all others. AI systems can quickly analyse large volumes of data, detect patterns and anomalies, and continuously learn, making them highly efficient in identifying sophisticated fraud schemes.

2. Data Analytics Platforms

- **Effectiveness: 75%**
- **Interpretation:**

  These platforms use statistical methods and trend analysis to uncover irregularities. They are quite effective, especially when integrated with business intelligence systems, and help uncover financial and operational data fraud.

3. Digital Forensics Software

- **Effectiveness: 70%**
- **Interpretation:**

These tools are primarily used to retrieve and analyse digital evidence from devices or networks. While still strong, their effectiveness is slightly lower, and they are often used in **post-incident investigations** rather than **real-time detection**.

4. Traditional Auditing Software

- **Effectiveness: 60%**
- **Interpretation:**

This tool is the least effective among the compared tools. Traditional methods focus on historical data and sampling techniques, which may miss subtle or complex fraud indicators, especially in modern digital environments.

Key Insights:

- **AI leads** in fraud detection efficiency, making it the most recommended tool for proactive monitoring and risk mitigation.
- **Technology adoption directly correlates with detection accuracy**—modern tools significantly outperform legacy systems.
- **Organisations aiming to strengthen their fraud detection frameworks should prioritise integrating AI and data analytics** into their audit and financial systems.

Conclusion:

Analytical tools and specialised software are crucial in modern forensic accounting, empowering professionals to conduct comprehensive and efficient investigations into financial discrepancies. Forensic accountants can effectively identify and examine instances of fraud by harnessing cutting-edge technologies such as data mining, machine learning, and artificial intelligence. These tools not only help capture anomalies in financial data but also allow for enhanced financial controls by providing insights into spending patterns and trends.

For example, forensic accountants may use visualisation tools to create detailed charts and graphs that depict unusual transactions or patterns, making it easier to spot fraudulent activities. Additionally, case studies reveal the real-world applicability of these technologies, showcasing instances where they have successfully uncovered fraud schemes and secured the integrity of organisations' financial practices. This data-driven approach strengthens trust with stakeholders and serves as credible evidence in legal proceedings when necessary. Overall, integrating advanced analytical tools in forensic accounting is essential for maintaining robust financial oversight and accountability.

Part 3

Applications of Forensic Accounting

Chapter 07

Forensic Accounting in Financial Crimes

"The Business Impact of Financial Crimes: Real Cases, Real Lessons"

Case Studies on Financial Fraud and Embezzlement

1. Enron Scandal

The **Enron scandal** was one of the most infamous corporate frauds in history. Here's a detailed background:

Formation and Rise of Enron

- **Formation**: Enron Corporation was formed in 1985 by merging Houston Natural Gas Company and InterNorth Incorporated. Kenneth Lay, the CEO of Houston Natural Gas, became the CEO of the newly formed Enron.
- **Transformation**: Under Lay's leadership, Enron transformed into an energy trading and utility company. The deregulation of the energy markets allowed Enron to trade extensively in energy derivatives1.

Key Figures

- **Kenneth Lay**: Founder and CEO of Enron.
- **Jeffrey Skilling**: Hired as the head of Enron Finance Corporation and later became the CEO.
- **Andrew Fastow**: Chief Financial Officer (CFO) who played a central role in using special purpose entities to hide debt.

Fraudulent Practices

- **Accounting Loopholes**: Enron used complex accounting practices, including mark-to-market accounting and special purpose entities, to hide its debts and inflate profits.
- **Misleading Financial Statements**: Executives misled the board of directors, the audit committee, and investors about the company's financial health.
- **Pressure on Auditors**: Enron pressured its auditor, Arthur Andersen, to ignore the issues and approve the financial statements.

Collapse and Bankruptcy

- **Public Exposure**: The fraud was discovered in October 2001, leading to a sharp decline in Enron's stock price.
- **Bankruptcy**: On December 2, 2001, Enron filed for Chapter 11 bankruptcy, which was the largest corporate bankruptcy in U.S. history at the time.
- **Legal Consequences**: Several Enron executives, including Skilling and Fastow, were indicted and sentenced to prison. Kenneth Lay was also indicted but died before sentencing.

Aftermath

- **Arthur Andersen**: The accounting firm was found guilty of destroying documents relevant to the investigation and lost its license to audit public companies.

Forensic Accounting Role:

1. **Detailed Financial Analysis:**
   - Forensic accountants analysed Enron's complex financial structures and transactions. They scrutinised the company's use of Special Purpose Entities (SPEs) and off-balance-sheet financing.

- They identified how Enron manipulated earnings through mark-to-market accounting, where future projected profits from trading contracts were recorded as actual earnings.

2. **Uncovering Irregularities:**

- Forensic accountants dug into Enron's accounting records, uncovering discrepancies between reported profits and the company's financial situation.
- They identified the role of key executives, like CFO Andrew Fastow, in creating fraudulent financial schemes to hide debt and inflate profits.

3. **Reporting and Testimony:**

- Forensic accountants provided detailed reports of their findings, which were used in legal proceedings.
- They testified in court, explaining Enron's complex financial manipulations and true financial state.

2. Bernie Madoff Ponzi Scheme

Bernard Lawrence "Bernie" Madoff was an American financier who orchestrated the largest Ponzi scheme in history, defrauding thousands of investors from an estimated $65 billion over several decades.

Early Life and Career

- **Born:** April 29, 1938, in Queens, New York.
- **Education:** Earned a degree in political science from Hofstra University in 1960 and briefly attended Brooklyn Law School.
- **Career Beginnings:** Bernard L. Madoff Investment Securities LLC was founded in 1960, initially focusing on penny stocks. Madoff's firm eventually became one of the top market makers on Wall Street.

The Ponzi Scheme

- **Mechanism**: Madoff's scheme involved paying returns to earlier investors using the capital from newer investors rather than profit earned by operating a legitimate business.
- **Deception**: Madoff created a facade of respectability and exclusivity, attracting wealthy and influential investors. He claimed to use a legitimate investment strategy called "split-strike conversion," which purportedly generated consistent returns.
- **Duration**: The scheme ran for decades, with Madoff admitting that it began in the early 1990s, although some evidence suggests it may have started as early as the 1970s.

Discovery and Collapse

- **Whistleblower**: Financial analyst Harry Markopolos repeatedly warned the SEC about Madoff's operations, but his warnings were ignored for years.
- **Revelation**: The scheme unravelled in December 2008 when Madoff's sons, Mark and Andrew, alerted authorities after their father confessed. Madoff was arrested on December 11, 2008.
- **Legal Proceedings**: On March 12, 2009, Madoff pleaded guilty to 11 federal felonies, including securities fraud, wire fraud, and money laundering. On June 29, 2009, he was sentenced to 150 years in prison.

Impact and Aftermath

- **Investor Losses**: The total amount missing from client accounts, including fabricated gains, was nearly $65 billion. Many investors lost their life savings.
- **Regulatory Failures**: The SEC was heavily criticised for failing to investigate Madoff more thoroughly despite numerous red flags and warnings.
- **Family and Associates**: Several of Madoff's family members and associates were implicated. His brother Peter was sentenced to

10 years in prison, and his son Mark died by suicide two years after Madoff's arrest.

- **Madoff's Death**: Bernie Madoff died in prison on April 14, 2021, at 82.

Legacy

The Bernie Madoff Ponzi scheme remains a stark reminder of the financial industry's importance of regulatory oversight and due diligence. It led to increased scrutiny of investment practices and reforms aimed at preventing similar frauds in the future.

Forensic Accounting Role:

1. **Transaction Analysis:**

- Forensic accountants thoroughly reviewed Madoff's financial records, tracing the flow of funds and identifying the use of new investors' money to pay returns to earlier investors.
- They scrutinised bank records, investment statements, and other financial documents to uncover the fraudulent transactions.

2. **Pattern Identification:**

- They used forensic analysis tools to identify patterns of fraudulent behaviour, such as consistent returns that were unusually high and lacked the volatility expected in legitimate investments.
- Forensic accountants reviewed the investment strategy Madoff claimed to use, discovering that the trades Madoff reported did not match market activity.

3. **Evidence Compilation:**

- They compiled detailed evidence that illustrated the scope and mechanics of the Ponzi scheme.
- Their findings were instrumental in the prosecution of Bernie Madoff, providing clear, concise explanations of the fraudulent activities.

3. WorldCom Scandal

Background of the WorldCom Scandal

The **WorldCom scandal** was one of the largest accounting frauds in history, leading to the company's bankruptcy in 2002. Here's a detailed overview:

Formation and Rise of WorldCom

- **Formation:** WorldCom was founded in 1983 by Murray Waldron, William Rector, and Bernard Ebbers as Long Distance Discount Services, Inc. The company initially focused on providing discount long-distance services.
- **Growth:** Under the leadership of Bernard Ebbers, WorldCom pursued an aggressive acquisition strategy, acquiring several telecommunications companies, including MCI Communications in 1998. By 2001, WorldCom handled half of all internet and email traffic in the U.S3.

Fraudulent Practices

- **Accounting Manipulation:** From 1999 to 2002, senior executives at WorldCom, led by CEO Bernard Ebbers, orchestrated a scheme to inflate earnings to maintain the company's stock price. They classified operating expenses as capital expenditures, which artificially inflated profits.
- **Discovery:** The fraud was uncovered in June 2002 by the company's internal audit unit, led by Cynthia Cooper. They discovered over $3.8 billion in fraudulent balance sheet entries1.
- **Extent of Fraud:** Eventually, WorldCom admitted to overstating its assets by over $11 billion, making it the largest accounting fraud in American history.

Collapse and Bankruptcy

- **Public Exposure:** The scandal came to light in the summer of 2002, leading to a sharp decline in WorldCom's stock price.

- **Bankruptcy**: On July 21, 2002, WorldCom filed for Chapter 11 bankruptcy protection. It was one of the largest bankruptcies in U.S. history.
- **Legal Consequences**: Several key figures were indicted and sentenced to prison, including CEO Bernard Ebbers and CFO Scott Sullivan. Ebbers received a 25-year prison sentence, while Sullivan received five years.

Aftermath

- **Rebranding and Sale**: WorldCom emerged from bankruptcy, rebranded as MCI Inc., and eventually sold its network assets to Verizon.
- **Regulatory Impact**: The scandal led to increased scrutiny of corporate accounting practices and contributed to the passage of the Sarbanes-Oxley Act in 2002, which aimed to improve corporate governance and financial transparency.

The WorldCom scandal serves as a stark reminder of the importance of ethical accounting practices and the potential consequences of corporate fraud.

Forensic Accounting Role

1. **Expense Examination**:

   - Forensic accountants investigated the capitalisation of operating expenses as capital expenditures. This practice allowed WorldCom to spread costs over many years, inflating profits in the short term.
   - They reviewed the company's financial records, identifying specific entries where expenses were improperly classified.

2. **Data Validation**:

   - Using forensic accounting software, they validated the data and identified discrepancies between reported financial figures and actual operational data.

- They cross-referenced WorldCom's reported financial performance with industry benchmarks and historical data.

3. **Internal Audit and Reporting**:

- Forensic accountants worked with internal audit teams to document the fraudulent activities. Cynthia Cooper, the head of internal audit at WorldCom, played a significant role in uncovering the fraud.
- They provided detailed reports and testified in legal proceedings, explaining the fraudulent accounting practices and their impact on WorldCom's financial statements.

4. **FTX Cryptocurrency Fraud**

Background of the FTX Cryptocurrency Fraud

The **FTX Cryptocurrency Fraud** was a major financial scandal involving the cryptocurrency exchange FTX, founded by Sam Bankman-Fried in 2019. Here's a detailed overview:

Formation and Rise of FTX

- **Formation**: FTX was founded by Sam Bankman-Fried and Gary Wang in 2019 as a cryptocurrency exchange and crypto hedge fund.
- **Growth**: FTX quickly became one of the largest cryptocurrency exchanges, handling billions of dollars in transactions. At its peak, FTX had over one million users and was the third-largest cryptocurrency exchange by volume.

Fraudulent Practices

- **Misuse of Funds**: Bankman-Fried diverted customer funds from FTX to his privately held crypto hedge fund, Alameda Research. He concealed this diversion from investors, falsely promoting FTX as a safe and responsible platform.

- **Special Treatment**: Alameda Research received special treatment on the FTX platform, including a virtually unlimited line of credit funded by customer deposits.
- **Overvalued Assets**: Alameda held significant holdings of overvalued, illiquid assets, such as FTX-affiliated tokens, which posed undisclosed risks to FTX customers.
- **Misuse of Funds**: Bankman-Fried used customer funds for various purposes, including investments in other businesses, real estate ventures, political donations, and charitable contributions.

Discovery and Collapse

- **Public Exposure**: The fraud was exposed in November 2022 when a news article revealed the extent of the financial mismanagement. This led to a surge in customer withdrawals and concerns about the company's stability.
- **Bankruptcy**: FTX filed for Chapter 11 bankruptcy protection on November 11, 2022.
- **Legal Proceedings**: Bankman-Fried was arrested in December 2022 and later extradited to the U.S. He was convicted on multiple charges, including fraud and money laundering, and sentenced to 25 years in prison.

Role of Forensic Accountants in Discovering the Fraud

Forensic accountants played a crucial role in uncovering the FTX fraud. Here's how they contributed:

1. **Financial Analysis**: Forensic accountants meticulously analysed FTX's financial records, tracing the flow of funds and identifying discrepancies between reported figures and actual transactions.
2. **Transaction Tracing**: They used forensic accounting techniques to trace the movement of customer funds from FTX to Alameda Research and other entities.

3. **Evidence Compilation:** Forensic accountants compiled detailed evidence of the misuse of funds, including specific transactions that could not have been completed without dipping into customer funds.

4. **Testimony**: They provided expert testimony in court, explaining Bankman-Fried's complex financial web and substantiating the prosecution's claims.

Forensic accountants' expertise in analysing financial data and identifying irregularities was instrumental in exposing the FTX fraud and aiding in prosecuting those responsible.

Strategies for Investigation and Prosecution

1. **Initial Assessment**

Identify the scope of the investigation:

- **Review Allegations**: Understand the specific nature of the allegations or suspicions that triggered the investigation. This could include fraud, embezzlement, financial misconduct, or irregularities.
- **Determine Investigation Goals**: Establish what needs to be achieved through the investigation. This involves identifying the specific frauds or irregularities that need to be proven and understanding the extent of the potential damage or loss.
- **Stakeholder Identification**: Identify all relevant parties involved. This includes employees, management, customers, vendors, and any third parties connected to the case.

Gather preliminary information and evidence:

- **Document Collection**: Collect initial documents such as financial statements, bank records, transaction records, emails, contracts, and other relevant records that might provide context or evidence.

- **Background Checks**: Perform background checks on key individuals involved in the investigation to understand their history and potential connections to the case.
- **Initial Analysis**: Conduct a preliminary analysis of the gathered documents to identify obvious discrepancies or irregularities that warrant deeper investigation.

2. Planning

Develop an investigation plan:

- **Outline Investigation Steps**: Clearly outline the steps to be taken during the investigation, including the methodologies and tools (e.g., forensic accounting software, data analytics, interview techniques).
- **Establish Timeline**: Create a detailed timeline for each investigation phase, including key milestones and deadlines.
- **Define Roles and Responsibilities**: Identify key personnel involved in the investigation, define their roles, and assign specific tasks based on their expertise.

Assign tasks and resources:

- **Resource Allocation**: Ensure that sufficient resources, such as forensic accountants, IT specialists, legal advisors, and any necessary external experts, are allocated to the investigation.
- **Task Distribution**: Allocate specific tasks to team members, ensuring that each task matches the most qualified individual.

Set timelines and milestones:

- **Milestone Definition**: Define critical milestones and deliverables for the investigation. These could include initial findings reports, interim updates, and final reports.
- **Progress Tracking**: Use project management tools to track progress against the established timeline and promptly address any delays or obstacles.

3. Data Collection

Collect relevant financial records and documents:

- **Financial Documents**: Obtain and review various financial documents, including general ledgers, accounts payable/receivable, payroll records, and expense reports.
- **Bank Records**: To trace the flow of funds, collect bank statements, check copies, wire transfer records, and credit card statements.
- **Contracts and Agreements**: Review contracts, purchase orders, sales agreements, and other binding agreements to understand the context of transactions.

Conduct interviews with key personnel:

- **Interview Planning**: Plan and prepare for interviews with key personnel, ensuring a structured and consistent approach to gather relevant information.
- **Interview Execution**: Conduct interviews to gather firsthand information, corroborate evidence, and obtain witness statements. Document all interviews thoroughly.
- **Follow-Up Interviews**: Conduct follow-up interviews as necessary to clarify inconsistencies, gather additional information, or explore new leads.

Obtain electronic evidence (emails, digital records):

- **Data Preservation**: Use forensic tools to collect and preserve digital evidence, ensuring the integrity and authenticity of the data.
- **Email and Communication Analysis**: Retrieve and analyse emails, messages, and other electronic communications for relevant information.
- **Digital Records**: Collect digital records such as logs from accounting software, ERP system data, and other electronic transaction records.

4. Data Analysis

Analyse financial transactions for anomalies:

- **Transaction Review**: Review individual transactions for unusual amounts, frequencies, or patterns that deviate from the norm.
- **Comparative Analysis**: Compare current transactions against historical data, industry benchmarks, and known legitimate activities to identify discrepancies.

Use forensic accounting software (e.g., IDEA, ACL Analytics):

- **Data Analytics**: Utilize forensic accounting software to perform advanced data analytics, such as Benford's Law analysis, ratio analysis, and anomaly detection.
- **Visualisation Tools**: Create visual representations of data, such as graphs and charts, to identify trends and patterns that may indicate fraud.

Identify patterns and trends:

- **Pattern Recognition**: Use data mining and machine learning techniques to identify recurring patterns that may suggest fraudulent activity.
- **Behavioural Analysis**: Analyse the behaviour of individuals involved in financial transactions, looking for red flags such as changes in spending habits, frequent use of cash, or irregular working hours.

5. Hypothesis Formation

Formulate hypotheses based on initial findings:

- **Hypothesis Development**: Based on initial findings and analysis, develop hypotheses about the nature and extent of the fraud.
- **Scenario Building**: Create scenarios that explain the observed anomalies and irregularities. Consider multiple hypotheses to explore different potential explanations.

Test hypotheses through further data analysis:

- **Validation**: Test the hypotheses by conducting further analysis and corroborating findings with additional evidence. Use statistical techniques and data validation methods to confirm or refute the hypotheses.
- **Refinement**: Refine the hypotheses as new data and evidence are uncovered, ensuring a thorough and accurate understanding of the fraud.

6. Evidence Preservation

Secure and preserve all collected evidence:

- **Evidence Storage**: Store physical and digital evidence in a secure, tamper-proof environment. Protect evidence with secure containers, locked storage rooms, and encrypted digital storage.
- **Documentation**: Document all steps taken to collect, handle, and store evidence, ensuring transparency and accountability. Maintain detailed records of who accessed the evidence and when.

Maintain a chain of custody for legal purposes:

- **Chain of Custody Records**: Maintain detailed records of the chain of custody, documenting every person who handled the evidence, when it was transferred, and for what purpose.
- **Legal Compliance**: Ensure that all evidence collection and handling procedures comply with legal and regulatory requirements to avoid any challenges to the admissibility of the evidence in court.

7. Reporting

Compile findings into a comprehensive report:

- **Report Structure**: The report should be structured with an executive summary, introduction, methodology, findings, analysis, and conclusion. It should also be logically organized and easy to follow.

- **Detailed Analysis**: Provide a detailed analysis of the findings, including charts, graphs, and tables to support the conclusions. Clearly explain the methods and techniques used in the investigation.

Include supporting documentation and evidence:

- **Supporting Materials**: Attach relevant documents, digital evidence, interview transcripts, and other supporting materials. Ensure that all evidence is properly referenced and organised.
- **Clear Presentation**: Ensure the report is clear, concise, and easy to understand. Use plain language and avoid jargon. Highlight key findings and conclusions.

8. Legal Proceedings

Present findings to legal authorities:

- **Presentation**: Present the findings and evidence to law enforcement, regulatory agencies, or legal counsel. Provide a clear and concise summary of the investigation and its findings.
- **Expert Testimony**: Be prepared to provide expert testimony in court to explain the findings and support the legal case. Clearly communicate complex financial concepts and evidence.

Assist in the prosecution process:

- **Collaboration**: Work closely with legal teams to develop the prosecution strategy. Provide additional information, analysis, and expert insights as needed.
- **Ongoing Support**: Provide ongoing support throughout the legal process, including responding to inquiries, preparing additional reports, and assisting with trial preparation.

Provide expert witness testimony if required:

- **Court Testimony**: Testify in court as an expert witness, explaining the investigation findings and providing insights into the financial aspects of the case. Use clear and concise language to communicate effectively with judges and juries.
- **Clarification**: Answer questions from attorneys, judges, and juries. Be prepared to clarify complex financial concepts and evidence to ensure a clear understanding.

9. **Follow-Up**

Monitor the case progress:

- **Case Updates**: Stay informed about the status of the case and any developments. Monitor the progress of legal proceedings and any related actions.
- **Ongoing Involvement**: Provide additional information and support as needed. Be available to respond to inquiries and provide further analysis or evidence.

Provide additional support as needed:

- **Post-Investigation Activities**: Assist with post-investigation activities, such as recovering assets, implementing fraud prevention measures, or training employees.
- **Recommendations**: Improve internal controls, enhance compliance, and prevent future fraud. Also, guide best practices and risk management strategies.

Chart Analysis: Growth in Investigation by Type Over Time (2010–2023)

This multi-bar chart presents the **number of fraud-related investigations** over four time points—**2010, 2015, 2020, and 2023**—categorised by the **type of fraud:**

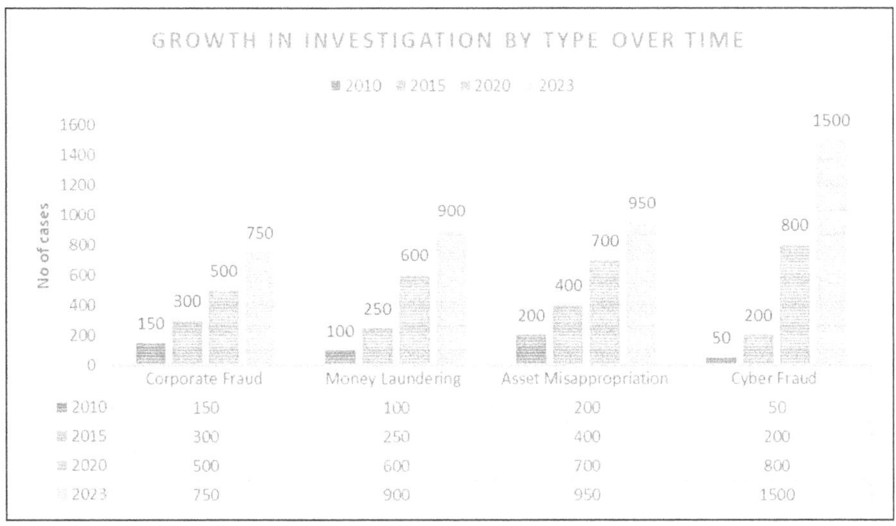

	Corporate Fraud	Money Laundering	Asset Misappropriation	Cyber Fraud
2010	150	100	200	50
2015	300	250	400	200
2020	500	600	700	800
2023	750	900	950	1500

Key Trends & Observations:

1. Cyber Fraud

- **2010:** 50 cases
- **2023:** 1500 cases
- **Growth: 30× increase**

  Insight: This category saw the **most explosive growth**, reflecting the rapid digitization of systems and the rise in cybercrime. Cyber fraud has become the **top investigative priority** in recent years.

2. Asset Misappropriation

- **2010:** 200 cases
- **2023:** 950 cases
- **Growth:** 4.75×

  Insight: Continues to be a **persistent threat** across industries. Though not as fast-growing as cyber fraud, it's still one of the **most common** fraud types under investigation.

3. Money Laundering

- **2010:** 100 cases
- **2023:** 900 cases
- **Growth:** 9×

  Insight: There's been a **significant rise in laundering investigations**, likely due to global efforts in tightening compliance and international AML regulations.

4. Corporate Fraud

- **2010:** 150 cases
- **2023:** 750 cases
- **Growth:** 5×

  Insight: Corporate fraud remains a **steady concern**, with governance and ethical breaches continuing to attract regulatory scrutiny.

Summary Insights:

- **Cyber Fraud is now the leading type of investigation**, indicating how digital vulnerabilities have outpaced traditional fraud mechanisms.
- **Money laundering and corporate fraud cases have surged**, likely driven by globalization, complex financial networks, and stricter regulatory audits.
- **Asset misappropriation**, while not the fastest-growing, still accounts for many **cases**, showing how internal controls and ethics remain a challenge.

Average Duration of Fraud Before Detection (in Months)

This bar chart compares how long different types of fraud typically go undetected, based on **average duration in months**:

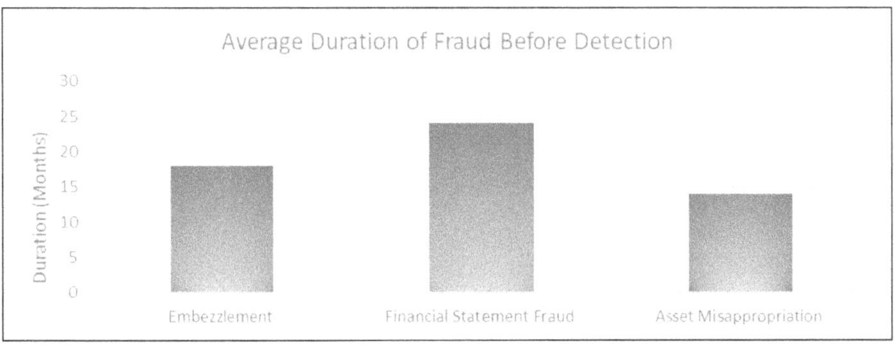

Breakdown by Fraud Type:

1. Financial Statement Fraud

- **Duration: 24 months**

  Insight: This type of fraud takes the **longest to detect**. Senior management often perpetrates it with access to complex systems, allowing them to manipulate financial reports and cover their tracks for extended periods. Detection often requires in-depth audits, whistleblowers, or regulatory scrutiny.

2. Embezzlement

- **Duration: 18 months**

  Insight: Embezzlement—typically involving the theft or misappropriation of funds by someone in a position of trust—can go unnoticed for over a year. These schemes often involve small but consistent amounts and internal collusion, making them **hard to detect with routine checks**.

3. Asset Misappropriation

- **Duration: 14 months**

  Insight: Although this is the **most common type of fraud**, it has the **shortest average duration before detection**. This may be due to:

- Regular audits and reconciliations catch anomalies
- More straightforward methods (e.g., theft of inventory or cash) that leave more unmistakable evidence
- Increased use of digital controls and inventory software

Summary Insights:

- **Longer Duration = Greater Risk:** The longer a fraud goes undetected, the more damaging it can be financially and reputationally.
- **Financial Statement Fraud poses the greatest hidden threat**, often causing **the largest losses** due to its scale and the perpetrators' level of authority.
- **Preventive measures such as internal audits, whistleblower policies, and advanced analytics** are key to reducing these durations and mitigating losses.

Conclusion:

Forensic accounting is indispensable in detecting and prosecuting financial crimes. These case studies and strategies highlight the critical role of forensic accounting in investigating and prosecuting financial crimes. Case studies illustrate the practical application of forensic accounting techniques, while strategies for investigation and prosecution show how forensic accountants contribute to justice. Through careful evidence gathering, collaboration with legal teams, and preventive recommendations, forensic accountants play a crucial role in safeguarding organisations against fraud. By understanding these processes, businesses can better protect themselves from fraud and ensure accountability.

Chapter 08

Role of Forensic Accountants in Legal Proceedings

"From Numbers to the Courtroom: Translating Data for Legal Success"

Forensic accountants play a crucial role in the legal process by uncovering the truth and promoting fair outcomes. They connect complex financial systems with the legal frameworks used to resolve disputes. Their expertise directly assists attorneys, courts, and clients in cases that the technical nature of financial evidence might complicate.

Introduction to Litigation Support in Forensic Accounting

The term "litigation support" refers to the process by which forensic accountants assist in preparing and resolving legal disputes. Their involvement begins before a case reaches the courtroom and often continues through the post-trial phases. Forensic accountants help uncover fraudulent activities, analyse damages, and ensure accurate financial reporting in financial disputes.

Forensic accountants possess specialized skills that enable them to untangle complex financial records. Their contributions extend beyond criminal cases; they also play a crucial role in civil litigation, regulatory inquiries, and arbitration. By presenting clear, evidence-based findings, forensic accountants ensure that legal decisions are grounded in financial accuracy.

Key Roles of Forensic Accountants in Legal Proceedings

The responsibilities of forensic accountants extend across multiple stages of the legal process. These roles are tailored to meet the unique demands of each case.

1.   Assisting Attorneys with Financial Evidence

Attorneys rely on forensic accountants to transform volumes of raw financial data into actionable insights. Financial evidence can be overwhelming due to its complexity, but forensic accountants simplify the information for legal teams.

- **Analysing Financial Data**: Forensic accountants scrutinise bank statements, financial ledgers, tax filings, and audit reports to extract relevant details.
- **Clarifying Transactions**: Forensic accountants help attorneys build narratives that align with the case's objectives by focusing on specific transactions. For example, in a fraud case, they may identify irregularities in fund transfers or unauthorised withdrawals.
- **Broader Context**: Legal disputes often involve nuanced financial frameworks. Forensic accountants explain the significance of financial evidence by using contextual understanding, such as industry norms or market trends.

This level of assistance allows attorneys to build compelling cases and address financial elements effectively during cross-examinations or arguments.

2.   Conducting Financial Analysis for Legal Claims

Forensic accountants play a pivotal role in analysing financial data to support or refute claims made by the parties involved in litigation. This analysis is crucial for quantifying damages or losses.

- **Fraud Investigation**: Forensic accountants investigate the flow of funds to detect signs of fraud. This may include uncovering fraudulent invoices, falsified financial statements, or money laundering activities.

- **Quantifying Losses**: Forensic accountants calculate the extent of monetary losses in cases of financial harm. For instance, in a breach of contract case, they determine lost profits resulting from the unfulfilled agreement.

- **Business Valuations**: Valuation services are critical in disputes involving mergers, acquisitions, or dissolutions of partnerships. Forensic accountants assess the value of businesses, real estate, intellectual property, and other assets to ensure equitable settlements.

These analyses are rooted in established methodologies and backed by robust evidence, making them reliable for legal proceedings.

3. Preparing Financial Documentation and Reports

One of the forensic accountants' defining strengths is their ability to present financial evidence in a clear, logical format. Reports prepared by these professionals often become the backbone of a legal argument.

- **Thorough Documentation**: Financial evidence is meticulously documented, indexed, and verified for accuracy, ensuring that no critical details are overlooked.

- **Authoritative Reports**: Forensic accountants prepare professional reports summarising their findings, methodologies, and conclusions drawn. These reports are written in a manner that is accessible to non-financial stakeholders, such as attorneys, judges, or jurors.

- **Court-Admissible Standards**: Financial documentation must adhere to strict legal standards. Forensic accountants ensure that their work meets these requirements, minimizing the risk of disputes over admissibility.

For example, in a shareholder dispute, a forensic accountant may prepare a detailed report showing financial discrepancies that justify a claim for damages.

4. Supporting Case Strategy Development

Forensic accountants are valuable collaborators during the strategic planning phase of litigation. Their insights shape the financial narrative of the case and help attorneys anticipate challenges.

- **Identifying Strengths and Weaknesses**: By reviewing financial evidence, forensic accountants highlight the case's strong points and areas that may require further substantiation.
- **Recommendations on Evidence**: They suggest additional documentation or data sources, such as supplementary audits or industry benchmarks, that can strengthen the case.
- **Countering Defence Arguments**: Forensic accountants predict opposing strategies and prepare counterarguments to address potential defences effectively.

This strategic input enables attorneys to present financial evidence with confidence and precision.

5. Providing Valuation Expertise in Disputes

Valuations are critical in many legal disputes, particularly those involving property, businesses, or marital assets. Forensic accountants provide unbiased and accurate valuations that form the basis for settlements or court judgments.

- **Business Valuations**: Forensic accountants determine a business's fair market value in cases of partnership dissolution or shareholder buyouts.
- **Asset Appraisal**: They assess the value of tangible assets like real estate, machinery, and inventory, as well as intangible assets such as patents, copyrights, and brand equity.

- **Supporting Fair Settlements**: Forensic accountants ensure that all valuations are transparent and supported by evidence, reducing the likelihood of disputes over fairness.

For instance, in a divorce case, a forensic accountant might calculate the value of a family-owned business to ensure an equitable division of assets.

Preparing for Court and Delivering Expert Testimony

Forensic accountants often testify as expert witnesses, where they must communicate their findings clearly and persuasively to judges, juries, and attorneys. Success in this role hinges on thorough preparation and effective presentation.

Preparing for Court

1. **Gathering and Organising Evidence**

The foundation of courtroom readiness is the meticulous organisation of financial evidence.

- **Thorough Review**: Forensic accountants examine all available records, ensuring accuracy and completeness. This includes reconciling inconsistencies or identifying gaps in documentation.
- **Simplification**: Complex data is broken down into key points, often supported by summaries or annotations highlighting its relevance to the case.
- **Cross-Referencing**: Evidence is systematically indexed to facilitate quick access during testimony or cross-examination.

2. **Preparing Reports and Summaries**

Reports and summaries serve as a roadmap for presenting findings in court.

- **Concise Writing**: Reports include an executive summary, detailed findings, and conclusions, ensuring that every element is clear and actionable.

- **Visual Aids**: Charts, graphs, and timelines are created to depict financial data visually, making it easier for non-experts to grasp complex concepts.
- **Professional Tone**: Reports maintain objectivity and avoid technical jargon, which enhances their credibility in a legal setting.

3. **Coordinating with Legal Teams**

Effective collaboration between forensic accountants and attorneys ensures alignment on case objectives.

- **Pre-Trial Discussions**: These meetings clarify how findings fit into the broader legal strategy and identify potential challenges.
- **Mock Trials**: Rehearsals allow forensic accountants to refine their delivery and anticipate cross-examination questions.
- **Strategic Input**: Forensic accountants provide insights that shape the attorney's line of questioning and courtroom presentation.

<u>**Delivering Expert Testimony**</u>

1. **Explaining Complex Financial Concepts**

Forensic accountants must distil intricate financial details into understandable terms for the court.

- **Simple Language**: Avoiding technical jargon ensures that even non-financial stakeholders can follow the argument.
- **Analogies and Examples**: Drawing parallels to everyday scenarios makes abstract concepts relatable.
- **Engaging Delivery**: Clear articulation of key points keeps the court's attention and reinforces the strength of the testimony.

2. **Presenting Findings Objectively and Confidently**

Objectivity is essential for maintaining credibility as an expert witness.

- **Neutral Perspective**: Forensic accountants present their findings without advocating for one side, focusing solely on the evidence.
- **Calm Demeanor**: Confidence, professionalism, and composure under pressure inspire trust from the court.

3. Using Visual Aids Effectively

Visual aids enhance the clarity and impact of financial evidence.

- **Simplifying Data**: Diagrams and graphs present key findings succinctly, eliminating the need for lengthy explanations.
- **Highlighting Patterns**: Visual tools can emphasize anomalies, trends, or the extent of financial damages.
- **Interactive Elements**: Forensic accountants can refer to visual aids during questioning, reinforcing their testimony.

4. Handling Cross-Examination

Cross-examination is a test of both technical knowledge and composure.

- **Preparation**: Anticipating opposing counsel's questions and rehearsing responses minimises surprises.
- **Maintaining Credibility**: Remaining calm and respectful under intense questioning prevents the witness from appearing defensive or biased.
- **Clarifying Misinterpretations**: Forensic accountants use opportunities during cross-examination to correct inaccuracies or clarify points of confusion.

Real-World Example

In a landmark corporate fraud case, forensic accountants uncovered a network of offshore accounts used to embezzle funds. Their expert testimony included transaction maps, digital evidence, and timelines that clearly illustrated the fraudulent scheme. Their objective presentation and well-supported findings were crucial in securing a conviction.

Forensic Accounting in Legal Proceedings: Criminal vs. Civil Cases

Forensic accountants play a pivotal role in criminal and civil litigation, providing expert analysis of financial data to uncover fraud, assess damages, and support legal arguments.

Criminal Cases

In criminal proceedings, forensic accountants assist in investigating financial crimes such as:

- **Fraud and Embezzlement**: Analysing financial records to detect misappropriation of funds.
- **Money Laundering**: Tracing illicit financial flows to uncover laundering activities.
- **Corruption and Bribery**: Examining transactions for evidence of corrupt practices.
- **Tax Evasion**: Identifying discrepancies in financial statements related to tax obligations.

For instance, forensic audits have been instrumental in India in cases like the Satyam scandal and the National Spot Exchange Ltd (NSEL) case, where forensic accountants uncovered significant financial irregularities, leading to legal action.

Civil Cases

In civil litigation, forensic accountants are engaged to:

- **Divorce Proceedings**: Valuing assets and uncovering hidden income or property.
- **Business Disputes**: Assessing financial damages and evaluating economic losses.
- **Shareholder Disputes**: Analysing financial statements to resolve conflicts among stakeholders.
- **Insurance Claims**: Validating the legitimacy of claims and quantifying losses.

Their expertise ensures accurate financial assessments, aiding in fair settlements and judgments.

Comparative Overview

While specific statistics on the number of court cases involving forensic accountants are limited, their involvement is crucial in both criminal and civil cases:

- **Criminal Cases:** Forensic accountants are essential in investigating and prosecuting financial crimes, providing evidence that can lead to convictions.
- **Civil Cases:** Their role is vital in resolving financial disputes, ensuring equitable outcomes based on thorough financial analysis.

Conclusion:

Forensic accountants are vital in legal proceedings, offering specialised knowledge for resolving complex financial disputes. Their expertise allows them to analyse and clarify intricate financial data, transforming it into accessible information for judges, lawyers, and juries. They play a significant role in shaping effective legal strategies by providing insights that can impact case outcomes. Additionally, they deliver compelling and credible testimony during trials, presenting their findings clearly and persuasively. By excelling in these responsibilities, forensic accountants contribute substantially to ensuring that court decisions are fair and based on a comprehensive understanding of the financial issues at play.

Chapter 09

Forensic Accounting in Corporate Governance

"Building a Fortress: Governance as Fraud Prevention"

Corporate governance is a complex framework comprised of specific rules, practices, and processes that guide a company's strategic direction and regulate its operational control. This comprehensive system is vital for cultivating trust among diverse stakeholders, including shareholders, employees, customers, and regulatory bodies. It ensures that organisations adhere to legal standards and ethical norms while maintaining the integrity and transparency of their financial operations.

In this landscape, forensic accounting plays a crucial role. This specialised discipline focuses on meticulously identifying vulnerabilities within financial systems, actively preventing fraud, and enforcing transparency in financial reporting and practices. Forensic accountants employ various techniques, from data analysis to investigative methods, to uncover discrepancies and safeguard against potential misconduct.

This chapter will examine the multifaceted contributions of forensic accountants to compliance, fraud prevention, and the development of robust internal control systems. These controls are essential safeguards designed to detect and deter financial irregularities, ultimately ensuring the organization's long-term sustainability and success.

Ensuring Compliance and Preventing Fraud

Introduction to Corporate Governance in Forensic Accounting

Corporate governance relies on accountability and transparency to protect the interests of stakeholders. Effective governance ensures compliance with laws, ethical practices, and industry standards while minimising the risks of financial irregularities.

Forensic accountants play a crucial role in achieving these objectives. By conducting audits, implementing fraud prevention measures, and ensuring compliance, they serve as guardians of an organization's financial integrity. Their expertise helps organisations foster a culture of accountability and ethical behaviour, which reduces the likelihood of legal penalties and reputational damage.

Importance of Forensic Accounting in Corporate Governance

Forensic accountants' contributions to corporate governance go beyond basic compliance. They provide comprehensive solutions that enhance the organization's financial health and foster stakeholder trust.

- **Protecting Stakeholders' Interests**: Forensic accountants safeguard the interests of shareholders, employees, and customers by preventing fraud and ensuring accurate financial reporting. Accurate financial records ensure investors make informed decisions.
- **Enhancing Transparency**: Honest and clear financial disclosures build confidence among regulators, investors, and the public. Forensic accountants ensure that all financial activities are reported truthfully.
- **Promoting Compliance**: Adherence to regulatory standards reduces the risk of fines, lawsuits, or loss of business reputation. Forensic accountants monitor compliance with laws like SOX (Sarbanes-Oxley Act), AML (Anti-Money Laundering regulations), and others.

Key Responsibilities of Forensic Accountants in Ensuring Compliance and Fraud Prevention

1. Conducting Compliance Audits

Compliance audits systematically evaluate an organization's adherence to regulations and standards.

- **Reviewing Financial Records**: Forensic accountants examine financial statements, internal reports, and regulatory filings to identify discrepancies.
- **Identifying Non-Compliance**: Audits detect areas where the organisation fails to meet regulatory requirements, minimising the risk of penalties. For example, an audit may uncover improper revenue recognition accounting.

2. Implementing Anti-Fraud Programs

Proactive fraud prevention measures are integral to effective corporate governance.

- **Policy Design**: Forensic accountants develop anti-fraud policies tailored to the organization's risk profile. These policies may address issues such as unauthorised access to accounts or misreporting of expenses.
- **Whistleblower Mechanisms**: Establishing anonymous reporting systems encourages employees to report suspicious activities without fear of retaliation.
- **Employee Training**: Awareness programs educate employees about fraud risks and their role in maintaining ethical practices. For example, training sessions may cover red flags for invoice fraud.

3. Regular Monitoring and Testing of Controls

Periodic assessments of financial controls ensure they remain effective.

- **Testing Control Mechanisms**: Forensic accountants simulate fraud scenarios to evaluate the efficacy of existing controls.

- **Identifying Weaknesses**: Regular reviews highlight vulnerabilities in processes, such as inadequate segregation of duties or outdated approval protocols.
- **Updating Controls**: Control update recommendations ensure that financial systems evolve with the organization's needs and industry standards.

4. Conducting Fraud Risk Assessments

Fraud risk assessments evaluate the likelihood of fraud within an organization's operations.

- **Identifying Risk Factors**: Forensic accountants assess risks based on industry trends, organizational structure, and transaction patterns. For instance, industries with high cash flow may be more vulnerable to skimming schemes.
- **Mitigation Plans**: Forensic accountants collaborate with management to develop strategies to address vulnerabilities, such as enhancing oversight for high-risk transactions.

5. Ensuring Regulatory Compliance

Compliance with regulations is a cornerstone of corporate governance.

- **Working with Compliance Teams**: Forensic accountants collaborate with compliance officers to align financial practices with legal requirements.
- **Adapting to Regulatory Changes**: They ensure that organisations stay updated on evolving regulations, minimising exposure to non-compliance risks.

Case Example: Compliance Audit Uncovers Internal Fraud

During a routine compliance audit, a mid-sized company discovered unauthorised vendor payments. A forensic accountant investigated the matter and found that an employee had created a fake vendor account to misappropriate payments over several years. The audit prevented further losses and resulted in improved vendor approval protocols, including a multi-level authorisation process for approving new vendors.

Building a Robust Internal Control System

The Role of Internal Controls in Corporate Governance

Internal controls are systems to ensure financial integrity, protect assets, and prevent errors or fraud. They are crucial to corporate governance and promote accountability and ethical behaviour within organisations.

Forensic accountants are key in designing, testing, and maintaining effective internal controls. Their work enhances security, improves operational efficiency, and fosters stakeholder trust.

Key Components of a Strong Internal Control System

1. **Segregation of Duties**

Segregating responsibilities among employees reduces the risk of fraud.

- **Dividing Roles**: For example, the employee responsible for approving payments should not also reconcile bank accounts.
- **Fraud Prevention**: Divided responsibilities make it harder for individuals to commit unauthorised actions without detection.

2. **Authorisation and Approval Protocols**

Clear guidelines for transaction approvals prevent unauthorised spending.

- **Setting Approval Limits**: Forensic accountants help define thresholds for different authorisation levels, such as requiring managerial approval for purchases exceeding a specific amount.
- **Hierarchy Definition**: Approval protocols ensure adherence to organizational policies while maintaining efficiency.

3. Document Control and Record Keeping

Accurate documentation provides a clear audit trail.

- **Mandatory Documentation**: Every financial transaction is recorded and linked to supporting documents, such as invoices or purchase orders.
- **Falsified Record Prevention**: Forensic accountants design systems that detect irregularities, such as missing receipts or altered entries.

4. Regular Reconciliations

Reconciliation ensures that financial records are accurate and consistent.

- **Bank Account Reconciliation**: Comparing internal records with bank statements helps identify unauthorised transactions.
- **Timely Corrections**: Regular reconciliations prevent errors or fraud from accumulating over time.

5. Employee Training and Awareness

A well-informed workforce is essential for maintaining internal controls.

- **Fraud Awareness**: Training programs educate employees about common fraud schemes and their role in preventing them.
- **Compliance Policies**: Employees learn about internal controls and organizational policies, fostering a culture of accountability.

Forensic Accountants' Role in Designing and Testing Internal Controls

1. Control System Design

Forensic accountants use their expertise to create tailored control systems.

- **Risk Identification**: They assess an organization's vulnerabilities and design controls to address specific risks. For example, implementing dual approval for expense reimbursements minimises fraudulent claims.
- **Practical Solutions**: Controls are designed to be effective without disrupting operational efficiency.

2. Testing and Monitoring Controls

Controls must be regularly tested to ensure continued effectiveness.

- **Simulated Scenarios**: Forensic accountants use auditing tools to mimic fraud attempts, assessing whether existing controls detect and prevent these activities.
- **Updating Controls**: Recommendations for updates ensure controls evolve with new risks or organizational changes.

3. Adapting Controls to Organisational Changes

Growth or restructuring can introduce new risks that require updated controls.

- **Departmental Expansion**: Forensic accountants help integrate controls into new departments or processes.
- **Ongoing Compliance**: Their involvement ensures that internal controls remain aligned with corporate governance standards.

Case Example: Strengthening Internal Controls in a Financial Services Firm

After a financial services firm experienced a data breach, forensic accountants reviewed internal controls and recommended improvements. They implemented tighter access controls, mandatory approvals for high-value transactions, and comprehensive employee training on data security. These measures reduced fraud risk and restored client confidence in the firm's practices.

Conclusion:

Forensic accountants play a crucial role in promoting effective corporate governance. Ensuring compliance, preventing fraud, and establishing strong internal controls help organisations create secure and transparent systems that encourage ethical growth. Their expertise in identifying vulnerabilities, adapting controls, and advising on best practices enhances organisational strength and protects stakeholder trust.

Part 4

The Future of Forensic Accounting

Chapter 10

Emerging Trends and Challenges

"Staying Ahead in the Age of Cyber Threats and Digital Currencies"

Advancements in technology have transformed the field of forensic accounting, providing powerful tools that enhance data analysis, improve fraud detection, and facilitate case resolution. However, these advancements also introduce new complexities and risks, especially as digital transactions become more widespread and sophisticated. Forensic accounting is rapidly evolving, shaped by technological progress, changing regulatory environments, and the rise of digital currencies. This chapter examines the impact of these factors and discusses the future challenges and opportunities that professionals in this field will encounter.

1. Impact of Technology on Forensic Accounting

a. Big Data and Analytics

Big Data refers to a massive amount of structured and unstructured information that is too large and complex for traditional computers. This data originates from various sources, such as social media, websites, sensors, and business transactions.

Analytics is the process of examining this Big Data to identify useful patterns, trends, and insights that help businesses and organisations make better decisions.

In short, Big Data serves as the raw material (vast amounts of data), while Analytics is the tool (methods to interpret the data).

- **Applications in Forensic Accounting:**
    - Identifying hidden patterns in large datasets to detect fraud.
    - Enhancing risk assessment models by integrating diverse data sources (e.g., financial transactions, social media activities).
    - Leveraging predictive analytics to anticipate potential fraudulent activities.

b. **Artificial Intelligence (AI) and Machine Learning**

Artificial Intelligence (AI) in forensic audit and accounting refers to using advanced technology that mimics human intelligence to detect fraud, analyse financial data, and automate auditing processes. AI can process large volumes of transactions, identify irregular patterns, and flag suspicious activities much faster than traditional methods.

Machine Learning (ML) is a subset of AI that allows systems to learn from historical financial data and improve their fraud detection capabilities over time. By analysing past fraud cases, ML models can recognise hidden patterns and predict potential fraud risks before they occur.

c. **Blockchain Technology**

Blockchain is a secure digital ledger that records transactions in a decentralized and tamper-proof manner. Instead of storing data in a single central location, blockchain distributes it across multiple computers (nodes), making it nearly impossible to alter or hack.

How Blockchain Helps in Forensic Accounting & Auditing:

1. **Fraud Prevention & Detection** – Since blockchain records are immutable (cannot be altered or deleted), fraudulent activities such as financial misstatements, unauthorised transactions, and data manipulation become easier to detect.

2. **Real-Time Audit & Verification** – Transactions recorded on the blockchain are instantly verifiable, reducing the need for time-consuming reconciliations and manual audits.
3. **Enhanced Transparency & Traceability** – Every transaction has a digital signature, timestamp, and audit trail, making tracking the flow of funds and uncover suspicious activities easier.
4. **Smart Contracts for Compliance** – Automated self-executing contracts ensure that financial and regulatory compliance rules are met without manual intervention, reducing the risk of financial misreporting.
5. **Forensic Investigations & Evidence Preservation** – Blockchain provides cryptographic proof of all transactions, helping forensic accountants collect undisputed evidence for investigations, litigation, and regulatory compliance.

In Simple Terms:

Blockchain acts as a secure, unchangeable, and transparent digital ledger, making forensic auditing more efficient by preventing fraud, ensuring data integrity, and allowing real-time verification of financial transactions.

d. **Robotic Process Automation (RPA)**

Robotic Process Automation (RPA) refers to using software "robots" or digital tools to automate repetitive, rule-based tasks traditionally performed by humans. In forensic accounting and auditing, RPA helps streamline data-heavy processes, improve accuracy, and speed up investigations.

How RPA Helps in Forensic Accounting & Audit:

a. **Automated Data Collection**

RPA bots can quickly extract financial data from multiple systems (ERP, bank statements, invoices, etc.) without errors, saving time in fraud investigations.

b. **Transaction Monitoring & Matching**

Bots can automatically scan thousands of transactions to identify mismatches, duplicate payments, or unusual patterns that may indicate fraud.

c. **Evidence Compilation**

RPA helps collect, organize, and document financial records systematically, which supports audit trails and legal evidence in forensic cases.

d. **Regulatory Compliance Checks**

RPA can automatically review compliance with laws, rules, and internal policies, flagging non-compliant transactions instantly.

e. **Real-Time Alerts**

Bots can be programmed to send alerts when suspicious or high-risk activity is detected in financial data.

In Simple Terms:

RPA in forensic accounting is like having digital assistants who work 24/7 to detect red flags, match records, and prepare clean, reliable evidence faster and without human error. It allows forensic auditors to focus more on analysing and interpreting results rather than spending time on manual tasks.

e. **Cybersecurity Tools**

Cybersecurity tools are technological solutions used in forensic accounting and auditing to protect financial data, detect cyber threats, and investigate digital fraud **or data breaches**. These tools help forensic accountants **secure sensitive information**, track unauthorised access, and gather **digital evidence** for investigations.

Key Roles of Cybersecurity Tools in Forensic Accounting & Audit:

1. **Data Protection**

   Tools like firewalls, encryption, and secure access controls protect financial records and accounting systems from unauthorised access or tampering.

2. **Threat Detection & Monitoring**

   Intrusion Detection Systems (IDS), Security Information and Event Management (SIEM), and anti-malware tools monitor networks and systems for suspicious behaviour or cyberattacks.

3. **Digital Forensics**

   Cybersecurity forensic tools (e.g., EnCase, FTK) help investigators retrieve deleted files, trace user activity, and preserve digital evidence for fraud cases and legal proceedings.

4. **Audit Trail Maintenance**

   Cyber tools log every user activity within financial systems, creating a reliable audit trail to detect who did what and when, which is crucial for investigations.

5. **Incident Response & Reporting**

   Cybersecurity frameworks help detect data breaches in real-time, contain damage, and document the incident for forensic and legal review.

In Simple Terms:

Cybersecurity tools function as digital bodyguards and detectives—they safeguard financial data from hackers, monitor for suspicious activity, and assist forensic accountants in tracing cyber frauds, recovering evidence, and ensuring systems are secure.

2. Rise of Digital Currencies and Their Implications

A. Growth of Cryptocurrencies

What Are Cryptocurrencies?

Cryptocurrencies, such as Bitcoin, Ethereum, and many others, are digital currencies that function independently of central banks or governments. They utilise blockchain technology as a secure and decentralised digital ledger.

How Have They Transformed Finance?

1. **Anonymity:**

    - People can send and receive cryptocurrencies without revealing their real identities.
    - This makes them appealing for legitimate uses and illegal activities such as money laundering, drug trafficking, and cybercrime.

2. **Decentralised Nature:**

    - There is no central authority controlling the system (like a central bank).
    - Transactions take place peer-to-peer using cryptographic protocols.
    - This makes it difficult for governments and law enforcement to monitor or regulate them effectively.

B. Challenges Posed by Cryptocurrencies

1. **Anonymity & Limited Regulation**

    - Cryptocurrencies use pseudonyms (wallet addresses) instead of real names.
    - Investigators can see transactions on the blockchain, but can't easily tell who owns what.

- Each country has different laws around cryptocurrencies, so no consistent international regulation exists.
- Criminals can exploit these gaps and move money across borders easily.

2. Stablecoins and DeFi (Decentralised Finance)

- Stablecoins (like USDT or USDC) are digital coins linked to real-world currencies (e.g., USD). They're meant to be stable in value.
  - However, many lack transparency, and often, there is no third-party audit verifying their backing assets.
- DeFi platforms let people borrow or trade crypto without using a bank or brokerage.
  - These platforms operate through automated smart contracts.
  - Because they're decentralized and often anonymous, they create new avenues for fraud and scams.

C. Tools Used in Cryptocurrency Investigations

1. Blockchain Analysis Tools

Forensic accountants and investigators now use advanced software to track crypto transactions:

- Chainalysis, Elliptic, CipherTrace: These tools help trace funds through the blockchain.
  - They can flag suspicious wallets, identify behaviour patterns, and help investigators link wallet addresses to real-world identities (where possible).

2. Collaboration with Law Enforcement

- Forensic professionals often work with cybercrime units and financial authorities.
- This collaboration is key to:

- Monitoring crypto exchanges (where people buy/sell crypto).
- Freezing or seizing suspicious wallets involved in criminal activity.
- Sharing intelligence globally to address cross-border crimes.

Summary

Key Concept	Simplified Explanation
Cryptocurrencies	Governments do not control digital money.
Anonymity	Hard to know who owns or sends crypto.
DeFi	Financial services without banks – more freedom, more risk.
Challenges	Tracking fraud is harder due to limited laws and anonymous users.
Tools	Blockchain analytics + global cooperation help track bad actors.

3. Future Challenges in Forensic Accounting

As forensic accounting becomes increasingly essential in combating financial crime, it encounters new and complex challenges that are technical but also legal, ethical, and global.

a. Evolving Fraud Tactics

Sophisticated Schemes

Fraudsters are becoming more tech-savvy. They use:

- Deepfakes (fake audio/video) to impersonate company officials.
- AI-generated invoices or emails to deceive staff and manipulate data.
- Malware or ransomware to steal or destroy financial records.

Example: A fake video could show a CEO authorising a money transfer, making it look authentic to accounting teams.

Globalised Fraud

Today's businesses operate across borders. Fraud does too:

- Money can move through multiple countries in minutes, using cryptocurrencies or offshore accounts.
- Different laws in each country make it harder to investigate and prosecute.

Challenge: Coordinating investigations across different legal systems and time zones can delay justice or let fraudsters escape.

b. Regulatory Adaptation

Laws Struggle to Keep Up

Governments are still catching up with:

- Crypto regulations
- AI and automated financial platforms
- New types of financial instruments

This makes it harder for forensic accountants to know what's allowed, what's grey, and what's illegal.

Example: Is a crypto transaction legal in one country but illegal in another? What if it crosses both?

Navigating Global Standards

Forensic accountants working internationally must understand:

- India's regulations (like PMLA, IT Act)
- Europe's GDPR and AML directives
- The U.S. Sarbanes-Oxley Act
- Differences in auditing and disclosure standards

Challenge: Mistakes in compliance can result in lawsuits or harm the reputation of forensic teams.

c. Talent Shortages

Rising Demand, Limited Supply

As fraud grows in complexity, so does the need for trained professionals. But:

- There aren't enough forensic accountants with knowledge in finance + law + tech.
- Universities are only recently adding digital forensics or AI ethics into their accounting programs.

Data Insight: In India alone, demand for forensic professionals has surged in banks, SEBI, and corporate governance roles — but many firms report difficulty hiring skilled people.

Need for Hybrid Skills

Today's fraud requires people who can:

- Read balance sheets
- Understand blockchain
- Follow court procedures
- Write investigation reports

Solution: Ongoing training and upskilling via certifications, industry mentorships, and simulation-based learning.

d. Ethical and Privacy Concerns

Balancing Detection with Privacy

Forensic tools collect data, sometimes personal or sensitive. But:

- India's PDP (Personal Data Protection) Bill and Europe's GDPR require explicit consent, security, and accountability.

- Companies can't "dig through emails or messages" without following protocols.

Risk: Overstepping can violate privacy, even if the intent was to detect fraud.

Misuse of Forensic Tools

AI tools can falsely flag someone as suspicious. Voice analysis or keystroke tracking might breach ethical boundaries.

Ethical Dilemma: Just because the tool can trace someone, should it? Especially if the person isn't convicted?

Final Thought

While the future of forensic accounting is bright with opportunities, it will only succeed if we:

- Stay ahead of fraud tactics.
- Align with evolving laws.
- Build diverse and skilled teams.
- Maintain ethical guardrails.

4. Future Opportunities in Forensic Accounting

Forensic accounting is no longer limited to fraud detection — it's evolving rapidly in response to new business, regulatory, and technological changes. Here's a closer look:

a. Expansion of Roles

- **From Detectives to Advisors:**

  Forensic accountants primarily detected fraud in the past. Now, they serve as trusted advisors, assisting organisations in building fraud-proof systems.

- **Governance & Risk Management:**

  They guide boards and top management on improving corporate governance and proactively managing business risks.

- **ESG Audits (Environmental, Social, Governance):**

  Companies are now evaluated not only for profits but also for their environmental and social responsibility. Forensic accountants help verify ESG data to ensure its accuracy and trustworthiness, preventing companies from making false claims..

Example: A forensic accountant might verify whether a company's "zero carbon emissions" claim is backed by facts or greenwashing.

b. Integration of Technology

- **Artificial Intelligence (AI):**

  AI tools can analyse thousands of transactions in seconds, detect suspicious patterns, and flag them instantly — tasks that used to take weeks manually.

- **Data Analytics:**

  Advanced analytics helps forensic accountants predict fraud risks before they occur by analysing trends, anomalies, and outliers.

- **Blockchain Technology:**

  Blockchain provides real-time, tamper-proof records. It's becoming especially valuable in sectors like healthcare, supply chain, and finance, where transparency is critical.

Example: In supply chain finance, blockchain can track every stage of a product, reducing billing fraud.

c. Collaboration Across Disciplines

- **Multi-disciplinary Teams:**

  Fraud today is not always just financial — it can be digital, legal, operational, or a mix. So forensic accountants are working with:

  - ➢ IT professionals (for cybercrime tracing)
  - ➢ Data scientists (for pattern recognition)
  - ➢ Lawyers (for litigation support)

- **Benefits of Collaboration:**

  This team approach improves investigation quality and accuracy, making presenting solid evidence in court easier.

Example: A cybercrime investigation might involve tracing money flows, hacking patterns, and legal compliance, all of which require diverse expertise.

d. Education and Training

- **Specialised Courses and Certifications:**
  Universities and institutes are offering:

  - Diplomas in digital forensics
  - Master's in forensic accounting
  - Certifications like CFE (Certified Fraud Examiner)

- **Continuous Learning is Key:**

  Due to rapidly evolving technology and regulations, even seasoned professionals enrol in online courses, workshops, and boot camps to stay sharp.

Example: A forensic accountant might attend a 2-day workshop on AI-powered fraud detection tools.

Forensic accounting is evolving from a niche skill to a strategic pillar in modern organisations. This field has significant growth potential, particularly for professionals integrating finance, technology, and legal expertise.

5. Case Studies: Technology and Digital Currencies in Forensic Accounting

In today's digital age, forensic accounting is no longer confined to paper trails and ledger books. With the emergence of cryptocurrencies and digital transactions, forensic accountants leverage cutting-edge tools like blockchain analysis and AI to track financial crime.

Let's examine some real-world case studies that highlight how technology is transforming the investigation and prevention of financial fraud.

Case Study 1: Blockchain-Based Fraud Detection in Supply Chain

Scenario:

A multinational manufacturing company noticed mismatched payments and duplicate invoices in its international supply chain network.

Investigation:

- Forensic accountants used blockchain analytics tools to trace the transaction history.
- They compared invoice data with blockchain-logged records.
- It was discovered that a rogue supplier was manipulating invoice data to receive duplicate payments.

Outcome:

- The company replaced manual approval processes with smart contracts — automated programs on blockchain that verify and authorise payments only if all conditions are met.
- Invoice frauds dropped by 85% within the first quarter of implementation.

Blockchain technology enhances transparency and automation in supply chains, enabling real-time detection and prevention of fraud.

Case Study 2: Cryptocurrency Money Laundering

Scenario:

A cyber fraud ring scammed victims online and laundered the proceeds using Bitcoin.

Investigation:

- Forensic accountants used tools like Chainalysis and Elliptic to track the movement of Bitcoin through different wallets.
- They identified "peeling chains" patterns — a common laundering technique where small amounts of cryptocurrency are peeled off and moved across multiple wallets.
- The trail led to crypto exchanges where Bitcoin was converted back to fiat currency.

Outcome:

- The fraudsters were caught, and millions in crypto assets were frozen.
- Authorities introduced enhanced monitoring and KYC protocols at crypto exchanges.

Takeaway: Cryptocurrency is traceable with the right tools, debunking the myth that it is entirely anonymous.

Case Study 3: Insider Trading Detected via Digital Footprints

Scenario:

A suspicious pattern in share price movements before major announcements raised red flags for a tech company on the stock exchange.

Investigation:

- Forensic accountants combined email surveillance, access logs, and stock trading data.
- AI detected correlations between internal file access and external trades.
- A mid-level employee was leaking confidential info to an external trader.

Outcome:

- Both the employee and the external trader were prosecuted for insider trading.
- The company introduced digital access audits and conflict-of-interest declarations.

Takeaway: Digital tools help trace financial and behavioural footprints that uncover white-collar crimes.

Case Study 4: DeFi Investment Scam

Scenario:

A group of Indian investors was lured into a "yield farming" DeFi platform promising 25% monthly returns.

Investigation:

- Forensic experts studied the smart contract code and found unauthorised fund redirection to private wallets.
- Blockchain tools revealed that the scammers used mixers and decentralised exchanges to obscure the trail.

Outcome:

- The platform was shut down, and the remaining assets were recovered.
- The case prompted SEBI to issue a warning on unregulated DeFi investments.

Takeaway: While DeFi offers innovation, it presents new fraud risks, requiring regulatory clarity and investor awareness.

Conclusion:

What These Cases Teach Us

Lesson	Explanation
Transparency Can Be Built	Blockchain doesn't just help in tracing — it can prevent fraud with real-time, unchangeable records.
AI and Pattern Detection is Key	Machine learning helps spot anomalies and red flags faster than manual checks.
Collaboration is Critical	Success in these cases involved coordination between forensic accountants, tech experts, and law enforcement.
Regulation Must Catch Up	Fraudsters are often one step ahead. However, organisations can stay protected by building robust digital infrastructure and policies.

6. Statistical Infographic for Impact and Challenges

Suggested Infographic Content:

- **Technological Adoption:** Pie chart showing the percentage of companies using AI, big data, blockchain, and cybersecurity tools in forensic accounting.

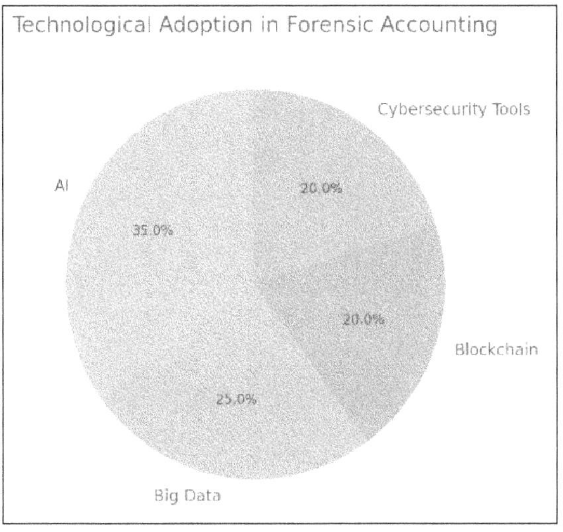

- **Fraud Trends by Sector:** A bar graph comparing fraud rates in the banking, healthcare, retail, and crypto industries.

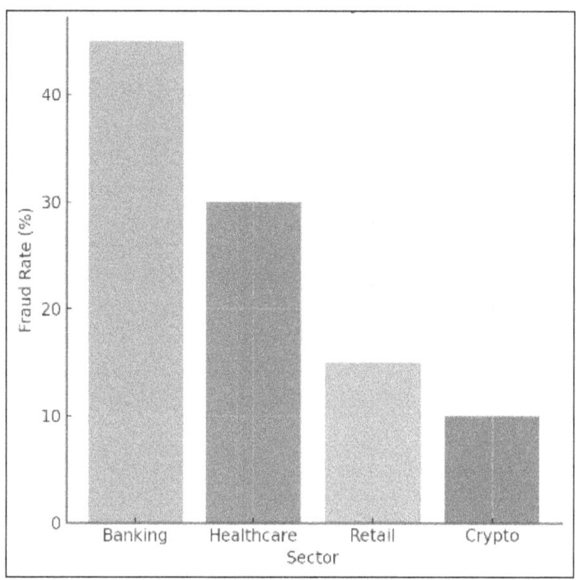

- **Crypto Fraud Growth:** Line graph showing the annual increase in cryptocurrency fraud losses.

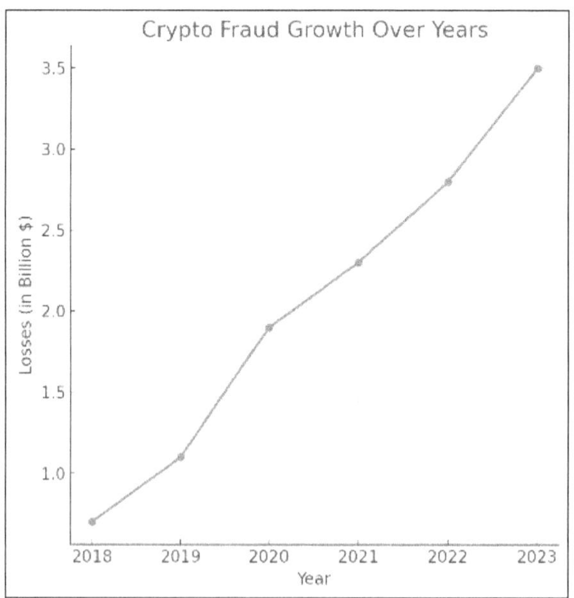

7. Conclusion

"From Insight to Integrity: The Journey of Forensic Accounting"

The future of forensic accounting lies at the intersection of technology, regulation, and human expertise. As fraud becomes more sophisticated and global, forensic accountants must adapt by embracing advanced tools, fostering interdisciplinary collaboration, and committing to continuous learning. By utilising new technologies, specialising in niche areas, and working alongside tech experts, forensic accountants can remain effective in an increasingly digital and interconnected world. By staying ahead of trends and challenges, they can uphold financial integrity and foster trust in a complex economic landscape.

As technology continues to evolve, forensic accounting is set for significant transformation. Emerging trends such as artificial intelligence, blockchain, and digital currencies present challenges and opportunities, requiring forensic accountants to adapt and innovate continuously. The future of forensic accounting will demand flexibility, specialised skills, and a proactive approach to navigate these complexities successfully.

Chapter 11

Conclusion

Recap of Key Concepts

Throughout this book, we explored the fundamental principles, techniques, and applications of forensic accounting, focusing on safeguarding business assets, preventing fraud, and conducting investigations to ensure financial integrity. We began with understanding forensic accounting's purpose and scope, distinguishing it from traditional accounting by emphasising its investigative and legal applications. From there, we delved into the critical skills and ethical responsibilities required of forensic accountants, highlighting the importance of integrity, objectivity, and professional skepticism.

We examined the essential techniques and tools forensic accountants use to detect, investigate, and prevent financial fraud. These methods include data analytics, interviewing techniques, and digital forensics, enabling forensic accountants to analyse complex financial data and identify irregularities. We also discussed the technological advancements reshaping forensic accounting, such as AI, big data, blockchain, and digital currency, each offering new opportunities and challenges in fraud detection and prevention.

Finally, we explored the practical applications of forensic accounting in corporate governance, litigation support, and fraud prevention, and how it assists organisations in maintaining compliance, establishing internal controls, and preparing for potential legal proceedings.

The Evolving Role of Forensic Accounting in Safeguarding Financial Integrity

Forensic accounting is no longer confined to post-fraud analysis; it now plays a proactive role in preventing financial misconduct and supporting sustainable business growth. As technology advances and financial transactions grow more complex, forensic accountants are at the forefront of innovation, developing new methods to tackle emerging cybercrime, cryptocurrency fraud, and global financial manipulation threats.

Forensic accountants are guardians of financial integrity in today's digital landscape. They help businesses navigate regulatory challenges, protect assets, and foster stakeholder trust. They are instrumental in building and reinforcing ethical, transparent financial practices, thereby contributing to a resilient financial ecosystem that promotes long-term success and stability.

As forensic accounting continues to evolve, so does its significance in the modern economy. With emerging trends shaping new demands and opportunities, forensic accountants must remain agile, continuously updating their skills and adapting to a rapidly changing environment. By embracing new technologies, deepening their knowledge of global financial systems, and upholding the highest ethical standards, forensic accountants are well-positioned to play a critical role in the future of financial security, helping businesses thrive in an increasingly complex and interconnected world.

This conclusion ties together the book's themes and emphasises the ongoing importance of forensic accounting in promoting financial integrity and protecting organisations in a dynamic economic landscape.

Are Frauds More Likely to Happen When We Move From 2x to 10x?

Yes, rapid growth—especially when moving from 2x to 10x- can increase the chances of fraud within an organisation. Growth brings excitement and opportunity, but also introduces a range of new risks. Here's how high-growth periods can inadvertently create an environment more susceptible to fraud:

1. Strain on Internal Controls

Fast expansion often puts pressure on existing systems and controls. A company may grow faster than its capacity to adapt to a governance framework, leaving gaps in oversight, security, and financial controls. Individuals motivated to commit fraud can exploit these gaps.

2. Increased Complexity and Volume of Transactions

When an organisation experiences exponential growth, its transaction volume and complexity increase significantly. This can make detecting irregularities or suspicious activity harder, as more transactions may go unchecked or unvouched. Fraudulent activities can more easily blend into a higher volume of financial data.

3. High-Pressure Environment

Rapid growth often creates a high-pressure work culture, with employees focused on ambitious targets, expansion milestones, and performance metrics. This environment can lead individuals to rationalise unethical behaviour, such as manipulating financial data or cutting corners to meet targets. The "pressure" component of the *Fraud Triangle* (Pressure, Opportunity, Rationalisation) becomes more pronounced under these circumstances.

4. New Hires and Limited Vetting

Organisations may hire quickly to keep up with growth, sometimes without thoroughly vetting new employees or adequately training them in the company's controls, policies, and ethical expectations. Employees unfamiliar with company procedures or potentially unchecked backgrounds can create a risk for fraud.

5. Less Focus on Governance and Compliance

In the excitement of rapid expansion, some organisations may prioritise revenue growth over compliance and governance. Leadership may overlook regular audits, internal control reviews, or compliance checks, focusing instead on scaling operations. This reduced focus on governance can inadvertently create opportunities for fraud.

6. Weakening of Organisational Culture

The pace of growth can dilute an organisation's culture, especially if new employees are brought on board faster than they can be integrated into the company's values and ethics. In a culture that hasn't firmly established a commitment to ethical practices, fraud can more easily take root as individuals feel less connected to the organisation's core values.

7. Increased Reliance on Technology and Automation

As organisations grow, they often adopt new technology and automation tools to manage the higher volume of transactions. If these systems are not secure, or if there's insufficient oversight of automated processes, they can be exploited to facilitate fraud, especially when security protocols lag behind the rapid implementation of new systems.

Preventing Fraud During Rapid Growth

To mitigate these risks, organisations can take specific steps as they scale up:

- **Strengthen Internal Controls**: Regularly assess and update controls to match the organisation's growth. This includes routine audits, transaction monitoring, and building checks and balances.

- **Implement Continuous Monitoring**: Use data analytics and fraud detection tools to monitor transactions, flag anomalies, and identify patterns indicative of fraud.
- **Foster a Strong Ethical Culture**: Reinforce the company's commitment to integrity and ethics, even during rapid change. Communicate values regularly and set a strong tone at the top.
- **Conduct Thorough Training**: Ensure all employees, particularly new hires, understand the organisation's controls, policies, and ethical standards.
- **Invest in Technology Security**: As technology grows within the company, ensure that cybersecurity and data protection measures are enhanced.

Rapid growth brings tremendous opportunity but requires a deliberate focus on maintaining a strong foundation of controls, ethics, and oversight. By proactively addressing these risks, organisations can reduce the likelihood of fraud while navigating periods of high growth.

Checklist for Fraud Prevention and Detection

Fraud prevention and detection require a proactive, systematic approach integrating robust internal controls, technological tools, and a culture of accountability. Below is a detailed checklist designed for businesses, auditors, and financial professionals to mitigate fraud risks effectively.

1. Governance and Leadership

☑ **Establish a Tone at the Top**

- Foster an organisational culture of ethics and transparency led by senior management.
- Set clear expectations for ethical behaviour through codes of conduct and compliance policies.

☑ **Board Oversight**

- Ensure the active involvement of the Board of Directors in overseeing fraud risks.
- Appoint an Audit Committee to monitor financial reporting and control systems.

☑ **Whistleblower Policy**

- Establish a confidential reporting mechanism for employees to report suspicious activities without fear of retaliation.

2. Risk Assessment and Planning

☑ **Conduct Regular Fraud Risk Assessments**

- Identify high-risk areas prone to fraud.
- Assess the likelihood and impact of possible fraud scenarios.

☑ **Develop a Fraud Response Plan**

- Create a documented plan to promptly and effectively address fraud incidents.

- Assign responsibilities for investigation and communication during fraud events incidentss.

3. Internal Controls

☑ Segregation of Duties

- Divide critical financial tasks among different employees to prevent unauthorised access.

☑ Access Controls

- Restrict access to financial systems and sensitive information to authorised personnel only.
- Use multi-factor authentication and strong password policies.

☑ Approval Processes

- Require dual or multi-level approval for high-value transactions, payments, and contracts.

☑ Reconciliation and Monitoring

- Perform regular bank reconciliations and review of key financial accounts.
- Use exception reports to identify unusual patterns or anomalies in transactions.

☑ Inventory and Asset Management

- Maintain a robust tracking system for physical assets and inventory.
- Conduct periodic audits to ensure accuracy and prevent asset misappropriation.

4. Employee Training and Awareness

☑ Fraud Awareness Programs

- Train employees on recognising red flags and understanding their roles in fraud prevention.

- Provide case studies and real-world examples to highlight the impact of fraud.

☑ Ethics Training

- Conduct regular sessions on ethical decision-making and corporate compliance.
- Emphasise the importance of accountability at all organisational levels.

5. Technological Tools and Data Analytics

☑ Fraud Detection Software

- Use AI-powered tools to identify anomalies, flag suspicious transactions, and analyse patterns.

☑ Continuous Monitoring

- Implement automated systems to monitor real-time transactions for irregularities.

☑ Data Analytics and Forensic Tools

- Use data visualisation tools to detect hidden trends or correlations indicative of fraud.
- Leverage blockchain technology for secure and transparent financial records.

6. Vendor and Third-Party Management

☑ Vendor Due Diligence

- Conduct background checks on suppliers, contractors, and other third parties.
- Verify credentials, financial stability, and reputation before onboarding.

☑ Contracts and Payment Reviews

- Use standardised contracts with clear terms to avoid disputes.

- Regularly review vendor invoices and payment records for discrepancies.

7. Fraud Detection and Investigation

☑ Red Flag Identification

- Monitor for common warning signs, such as:
- Unusual accounting entries.
- Frequent cash transactions.
- Sudden lifestyle changes of employees.

☑ Periodic Audits

- Schedule surprise and routine audits to verify compliance and detect irregularities.

☑ Investigation Protocols

- Establish procedures for initiating fraud investigations, preserving evidence, and interviewing witnesses.

8. Reporting and Legal Compliance

☑ Regulatory Adherence

- Stay updated on fraud prevention laws and standards relevant to your industry.
- Ensure compliance with anti-money laundering (AML) and anti-bribery regulations.

☑ Incident Reporting

- Report fraud incidents promptly to regulatory authorities and stakeholders.
- Document findings and corrective actions comprehensively.

9. Building a Fraud-Resistant Culture

☑ Encourage Ethical Behaviour

- Recognise and reward employees who uphold ethical standards.
- Ensure that no one, regardless of rank, is above accountability.

☑ Leadership Accountability

- Hold senior management accountable for lapses in internal controls or ethical violations.

10. Continuous Improvement

☑ Periodic Review of Policies

- Update fraud prevention and detection policies to reflect new risks and regulatory changes.

☑ Leverage Lessons Learned

- Analyse past fraud incidents to improve preventive measures.
- Share insights across departments to strengthen the organisation collectively.

Conclusion:

Fraud prevention and detection require vigilance, teamwork, and a commitment to maintaining the highest standards of financial integrity. This checklist serves as a roadmap for creating an environment where fraud is difficult to perpetrate and swiftly detected and addressed.

Sample Forensic Audit Report

Below is a sample Financial Forensic Audit Report involving employee fraud within an organisation. This is a general template you can modify according to the type of organisation, the nature of the fraud, and the level of detail you wish to include, keeping in mind the scope of the assignment.

Forensic Audit Report

To,
The Management
XYZ Manufacturing Pvt. Ltd.
New Delhi (INDIA)

Subject: Investigation into Alleged Employee Fraud
Audit Conducted By: [Your Name], Chartered Accountant, FAFD
Date of Report: [Insert Date]
Reporting Period Covered: April 1, 2022 – March 31, 2024

1. Executive Summary

This forensic audit was initiated in response to allegations of financial irregularities within the accounts department of XYZ Manufacturing Pvt. Ltd. The investigation focused on suspicious transactions, misappropriation of funds, and manipulation of vendor payments. The audit uncovered evidence of employee fraud involving unauthorized payments, creation of fictitious vendors, and falsification of financial records.

2. Objective of the Audit

- To investigate and identify the nature and extent of the suspected fraud
- To quantify the financial impact of the fraudulent activities
- To identify individuals involved and recommend actions
- To assess control weaknesses and suggest corrective measures

3. Scope of Work

- Review of accounting records and bank statements
- Examination of vendor master data and payment trails
- Interviews with relevant employees and management
- Use of forensic data analysis software to detect anomalies

4. Methodology

- Conducted transaction testing on high-value and high-frequency payments
- Performed digital forensics on emails and communication logs
- Verified supporting documents such as invoices, GRNs, and payment vouchers
- Cross-verified vendor bank accounts with employee information

5. Findings

a. Creation of Fictitious Vendors

- A total of **six fictitious vendors** were identified in the ERP system. (Annexure A)
- These vendors were created using personal email addresses and duplicate tax identification numbers.
- Payments totalling **INR 28.75 lakhs** were routed through these vendors over 14 months. (Annexure B)

b. Unauthorised Payments

- 22 payments, amounting to **INR 15.20 lakhs**, were made without proper invoice backing or purchase orders. (Annexure C)
- Audit trail revealed payments approved using forged digital signatures.

c. Employee Involvement

- Evidence points to the direct involvement of Mr. ABC (Senior Accounts Executive) and collusion with one junior staff member. (Annexure D)

- Mr. ABC used administrative privileges to alter vendor details and manipulate transaction logs. (Annexure E)

d. Lack of Controls

- No segregation of duties between vendor creation, payment approval, and bank reconciliation.
- Inadequate oversight of employee access rights and audit logs.

6. Quantification of Loss

The total financial loss due to fraudulent transactions has been quantified at **INR 43.95 lakhs**, excluding potential indirect losses such as reputation damage and legal costs. (Annexure F)

7. Recommendations

a. Disciplinary and Legal Action

- Immediate suspension of the involved employees pending a formal inquiry
- Filing of FIR and civil recovery proceedings

b. Strengthening Internal Controls

- Implementation of a maker-checker system for all payments
- Mandatory vendor due diligence before onboarding
- Restriction of user access based on role hierarchy

c. Monitoring and Prevention

- Periodic forensic reviews of high-risk areas
- Use of automated audit trail monitoring tools
- Staff training on ethics and fraud awareness

8. Conclusion

The forensic audit confirms that certain employees within the organisation executed a deliberate scheme of financial fraud by exploiting internal control weaknesses. Prompt corrective actions are critical to mitigating future risks and restoring the organization's financial integrity.

[Signature]
[Your Name]

[Date]

USEFUL LINKS FOR FURTHER STUDIES

https://www.britannica.com
https://en.wikipedia.org/wiki
https://www.icai.org/resources.shtml
https://www.icsi.edu/
https://sfio.gov.in/en/
https://www.sebi.gov.in/
https://enforcementdirectorate.gov.in/

Write to CA Satish Patel
casatishpatel@yahoo.in

Follow CA. Satish Patel on these channels

http://www.linkedin.com/in/satish-patel-954368243
https://www.youtube.com/@SATISHPATEL_P
https://www.youtube.com/channel/UC__0GJkBHlLQaWfSWIdVXHw
https://www.facebook.com/PatelNGupta/

About the Author

CA Satish Patel is a Chartered Accountant certified in Forensic Accounting and Fraud Detection (FAFD, ICAI). He has over 30 years of experience in taxation, auditing, accountancy, finance, and management consulting. Throughout his distinguished career, he has worked with businesses of all sizes, guiding them through complex financial matters, strengthening internal controls, and helping prevent fraud.

A recognised expert in forensic accounting, Patel combines deep analytical skills with practical insights to protect organisational assets and promote financial transparency. With a proven track record in fraud investigation, legal compliance, and risk management, he has played a key role in uncovering and preventing fraudulent schemes across diverse sectors.

Known for his pragmatic, ethical, and client-focused approach, the author has advised numerous organisations on governance improvements and fostering a culture of accountability. Passionate about sharing knowledge, he actively writes, teaches, and mentors, contributing to the development of future forensic professionals.

This book, *Financial Forensics Unleashed: Empowering Entrepreneurs, CEOs, Auditors, and Financial Experts to Detect and Prevent Fraud,* reflects decades of hands-on expertise and aims to equip readers with the tools and mindset to combat modern financial threats.

Abstract

This book serves as a comprehensive guide, structured to take readers through the fundamentals of forensic accounting, the specific techniques used to detect and investigate fraud, and the applications that can safeguard businesses. Whether you are a business owner looking to establish sound financial practices, a forensic accountant seeking to expand your skill set, or a consultant advising clients on risk management, you will find practical insights here to support your goals.

casatishpatel@yahoo.in

www.ingramcontent.com/pod-product-compliance
Lightning Source LLC
Chambersburg PA
CBHW040754120726
48005CB00012B/1167